WESTMAR COLL
W9-ARG-617

VOCAL RESONANCE

ITS SOURCE AND COMMAND

VOCAL RESONANCE

ITS SOURCE AND COMMAND

By

M. BARBEREUX-PARRY

The Christopher Publishing House
53 Billings Road
North Quincy, Mass. 02171

MT
825
.B25
1979

COPYRIGHT © 1941
BY THE CHRISTOPHER PUBLISHING HOUSE
COPYRIGHT © 1979
BY THE CHRISTOPHER PUBLISHING HOUSE

Library of Congress Catalog Card Number 79-50537

ISBN: 0–8158–0380–X

PRINTED IN
THE UNITED STATES OF AMERICA

96927

DEDICATION

Vocal expression is universal in its adaptation to human needs.

When vocal expression is liberated from physical sensation and adapted to the use of pure resonance alone, it becomes basic to the needs of educational unfoldment in every line and opens the way to unlimited capacity in every individual.

To each student of the BARBEREUX SYSTEM, whether past, present or future, this little book is lovingly dedicated.

VOCAL RESONANCE

ITS SOURCE AND COMMAND

PART I

PREFACE

A short resume of certain points of value in the unfoldment of the *Barbereux System,* which may be of interest to those who are following this plan of study.

The work is based on a discovery made by Madame Barbereux-Parry in 1894. Having been gifted with a natural talent for singing and a voice of much promise, after several years of vocal study with some of the most noted teachers of the times in Chicago, New York and Boston, she was stricken with an entire loss of voice; even the speech condition was seriously affected. She was crushed with disappointment for over a year, at the end of which time the inspiration came to her to devote her life to this cause, and if possible find a solution whereby no one else need ever pass through her experience. From that time she began an exhaustive analysis of voices of young children especially, for *never* in the history of voice development has the *child* voice as such been in any way proven to be the logical basis for the *adult* voice in its manner of production. She had a deep conviction that in the child voice and its *spontaneous* delivery might be found the *key* to the whole enigma.

In order to have access to a great variety of types

through the period from early childhood past the age of adolescence, she entered the field of Public School Music, in five small towns in the Middle West, including ten thousand children throughout the grades, and for nine years carried on the work of laboratory analysis and investigation with no assistance or interference; for at that time the weekly visits of a special teacher of music covered all the time given to the study.

In 1896, she made the discovery upon which is based the *Barbereux System of Voice Production and Educational Unfoldment.* In 1905 she published a little booklet, "The First Five Years In a New Method of Singing". This discovery, after a period of several years, she was able to verify and establish through the science of anatomy and dissection of the human skull. It is a region known to Materia Medica as the "Inter-osseous Spaces", and which *never* before, in *any* way has been associated with the voice or its production. Madame Parry was able to prove, through the development of her work, that this is the elemental source of resonance upon which the human voice depends for its *motive power.* There being *no sensation* connected with this activity, it has never been recognized in its deep significance up to the time of her discovery.

Within two years after this, Madame Parry, through its application to her own great need, was able to *restore* her own singing voice with over an octave of tones *added,* which was entirely new in her experience, and for over twenty years she used her voice for professional singing, with gratifying results. For her condition entirely proved the truth of her discovery, and her vocal theory which is based upon it. For eighteen years she carried on her work of private teaching and singing. In 1909 the opportunity came to open her studio in Chicago, which she felt would give a greater scope to the System. For over twenty years she carried on her teaching in one of the finest studios in the far-famed Fine Arts Building, where her students came to her from all parts of the United States. For eight or ten weeks each summer she travelled, lectured, and held summer schools in various cities from coast to coast. In 1915, she published a book, "Vocal Limitation and Its Elimination (The Voice a Stringed Instrument)". From this time she gave normal work and prepared teachers to carry on the *Barbereux System* in different parts of the country in private studios.

She had longed for many years to go back to the child voice and make more clear the fact that upon the *child consciousness* and its *spontaneous unfoldment* rests the *most advanced* educational movement of all time. In 1921 she purchased property in Evanston, Illinois, and erected a residence studio for the sole purpose of carrying on a laboratory school with children ranging from the age of seventeen months to four years. This school was carried on over a period of years, during which time she established complete courses of study in Pre-kindergarten, Kindergarten, Piano, Singing, Diction, Creative Interpretation (Dramatics) and Activity Release; also Correspondence Courses for mothers and teachers.

In 1930 Madame Parry gave up her studio in Chicago and has since spent her time in periods of intensive teaching in various centers. In 1934 she opened a studio in Los Angeles, from which center the work is now radiating.

In closing this sketch of a pioneer who has opened new paths in an unknown world of vocal tone and its close relationship to all singing, speech and *educational* endeavor, through a purely *mental* approach, it may be of interest to know a more personal phase of her experience and its bearing on her work.

In 1901 Madame Parry became the wife of a student of Materia Medica, who was then pursuing his course of study in Boston University, with whom for eighteen years she was closely associated in the development of his profession and the building of his practice. He chose the special realm of eye, ear, nose and throat, and became successful in his line.

The unfoldment of her own profession was thus through the understanding, basically, of all that Medical science and anatomical research had to offer at *that time*. While she attended summer courses with her husband given by great specialists in his line, in the clinics of Boston and New York, and afterwards spent four different periods of study in Europe, following research of specialists from Stockholm to Milan, from London to Vienna, she at the same time worked in her own line of voice and tone with Manuel Garcia in London; Vannini and Vanucini in Florence; Viardot-Garcia and Marchesi in Paris.

It was from out of this labyrinth of material knowledge she was able to emerge through the light of understanding with the full recognition of the fallibility of matter in its relationship to all endeavor, and establish the *Barbereux System of Educational Release and Unfoldment.*

To educate humanity in all lines of knowledge *apart* from the influence of materiality, we must begin aright.

When we lay aside will power, we lay aside resistance—without resistance there would be no physical sensation in any line of activity.

When all vocal expression becomes pure resonance, vocal tone is thus separated from the physical body via reflection, expanding in space without limitation. Singing thus becomes "Vocalized Speech" spontaneously expressed, as a bird sings, without the physical limitation of consciously directed breath, tone, register or pitch.

When *this* vision is adapted to *all* educational endeavor, we find that as the *will power ceases* to direct the human intellect, in its search for knowledge, (as in early childhood *before* we become conscious of self) thus, the highly sensitized state of the intuition will bring us all learning, and there will be no *obstruction* to the activity of the Creative Impulse and Inspiration. Thus, the imagination is constantly and constructively objectifying this unlimited supply; and all that is perfect, beautiful and true *becomes a reality* to us, *apart* from the influence of *wrong thinking.*

Following this plan, correct thinking is always spontaneous, affirmative and constructive, at all times *apart from self.*

CONTENTS

Vocal Resonance: Its Source and Command

PART I

Vocal Resonance

I

IMPRISONMENT

The first and most important requisite of any vision which can be applied practically to the needs of humanity at large, is that of a basic principle which can, through minute analysis, be proven fundamental and final. The fundamental principle upon which the *Barbereux System* is founded, is *Release.* Simply expressed, universal release means universal liberation—the antithesis of which is imprisonment.

The universal imprisonment of the human race as we find it today, can be traced to many causes, and is both physical and mental. Physical imprisonment finds its most fundamental cause to be a state of tension throughout the body, which is used in all forms of activity. This condition is primarily due to a belief in the necessity of making conscious the act of breathing, which in turn gradually readjusts the whole body to a false structural condition, the strain of which constantly holds the Solar Plexus (the sensory nerve center of the body) between the focal points of force and resistance.

To escape from *physical* imprisonment, the body must be adjusted to a new structural condition of support which releases all muscular activity from reactions in sensation (each set of muscles wholly independent in movement). This independence of each set of muscles can only be accomplished when we cease to depend upon the motivation of the human will. As long as one is dependent upon will power, all physical activity gradually becomes mechanized, and from this form of imprisonment there has been no means of liberation.

Mental imprisonment results, more or less, from all forms of education. The human mind is found to have unlimited capacity, but unless this capacity is adjusted to the activity of the creative impulse and the finer sensibilities, it also becomes mechanized, and true individuality cannot be expressed.

One of the saddest results of this state of human imprisonment, is that many times those individuals who are most talented, artistic and creative, in seeking to escape, are tempted to enter into the realm of the psychic and the occult, which can lead only to darkness and oblivion.

The universal key which will open the door of this mental and physical imprisonment of humanity, is found to be vocal expression. When all vocal expression is liberated from its dependence upon physical sensation and breath, it is thus connected with the activity of the creative impulse and the finer sensibilities, and is wholly in the realm of thought and inspiration.

As a result of this entire liberation of the individual from the drive of will power through which he has been imprisoned, all activity, physical and mental, leads to unfoldment, and through unfoldment he becomes more and more able to realize and take advantage of the unlimited resources of the universe.

II

EDUCATION

Prominent educators in all parts of the world are becoming aware of the great need of an entire readjustment of thought toward the *fundamentals* of education. They are also *beginning* to realize that this readjustment must include a *practical basis* for the recognition and unfoldment of the *creative feeling* within each individual. This change must be so fundamental in its influence upon the finer sensibilities and the intuitive feeling, that it will go *far deeper* than national or racial characteristics and tendencies, to a point which answers a *universal* need as well as an individual one.

The greatest obstacle that every individual must overcome in all lines of education, is some form of self-consciousness. The human family may be divided into two classes in their reactions to *this limitation.* The type who have the finer sensibilities, the temperamental and artistic, are the greatest victims. In proportion to the fineness of their nature and their artistic sense, self-consciousness gradually builds a wall about them which they are in no way capable of surmounting. They become the "round pegs in the square holes," a part of a great army who find no joy in daily work or living, since circumstances have closed for them the true medium of creative expression.

The other class is made up of those of coarser fibre and greater endurance, with which, in combating conditions successfully, they develop an inflated egotism which gradually dulls the finer sensibilities and the intuitive feelings. In this class are found many whom the world calls successful, though their lives are given over to a constant gratification of self and selfish ambition.

We can safely state that every work which has had *lasting* value in the progress of humanity, has come through *inspiration,* spontaneously and without conscious preparation—as a flash of light. He who *faithfully* follows a vision of *this* kind is shown the *perfection* of some idea which *transcends human concept.* Thus each step in the progress of humanity has been made through the intuitive feeling of one who is *prepared* to receive it. The basic value of education lies in its power to increase our understanding. In proportion to the increase of our understanding, we gain the vision which allows us to discern and follow that which is *true* in all lines of progress.

This new vision of education which is being considered in all parts of the world today is seeking to find a way through which education may bring to each individual an unfoldment of the *creative impulse.* In the *Barbereux System of Educational Unfoldment,* we believe there has been found a very *significant* approach to this ideal. This manner of awakening and liberating the creative impulse through the medium of vocal expression, is most practical and easy of application, for is not *speech* the most universal form of human expression? It comes from the deepest recesses of each individual nature. In proportion as this medium of vocal tone becomes entirely liberated, balanced and wholly spontaneous, is the individual made capable of expressing, through his speech, not only elemental feelings, but shades of feeling which prove the voice is most closely associated with the imagination and all the finer sensibilities of each nature. Only when the finer sensibilities are awakened to their fullest capacity through this manner of producing this type of vocal sound, do we find unlimited possibilities in the unfoldment of each individual, which may be applied to any and all lines of educational endeavor.

This form of mental activity *awakens* all the finer sensibilities including the imagination, and adjusts the thought to *intuitional guidance in all lines,* which leads to *inspiration.* An encouraging note found in this advanced vision of education is the proof given that it may be *universally* and *individually* applied at *any age.*

In the realm of human education, *thus far,* all progress is entirely dependent upon the activity of the human intellect, driven by the human will. Through this mode of procedure the individual gradually becomes *mechanized mentally and physically,* and is found incapable of attaining his true individuality, the unfoldment of which depends upon the *liberation* of the creative impulse.

In the comparison of the above vision of education to the form of education which has existed in the world for centuries, we can get a vivid picture of the type of imprisonment which the old form has brought to humanity down through the ages. As long as the *human will* is *depended* upon to furnish motivation for all physical and mental activity, which results in gradual imprisonment of the individual and all his faculties and possibilities, it is no wonder that within the last few years the world is gradually awakening to the need of a more advanced form of education, which we believe has been found and proved in the *Barbereux System of Educational Release and Unfoldment.*

III

THE FIRST TWELVE YEARS

Child Consciousness Basis For True Education

Through the *Barbereux System* we approach the unfoldment of the entire individual, spiritual, mental, physical, from a basis that has not been used in this way with this vision in any form of education or unfoldment before.

We do not say, "we go back to childhood" for our approach, because *this* approach has a beginning much more definite and fraught with a much deeper significance than that phrase can possibly convey. At the beginning of human life when we are first born, each and every normal child comes into the world with a gift, or gifts, an individual endowment.

Only Through Child Consciousness Can We Awaken Creative Impulse

This state of a young child is one that is wholly receptive to all and any impressions with which he may chance to be surrounded. Associated with this unlimited state of receptivity is the "creative impulse" which seems to supply the incentive for all activity. As long as the child consciousness is left in this state he will in all ways naturally (unconsciously) unfold.

Through the intuitive impressions the creative impulse is constantly supplied with all material necessary for its natural functioning. Closely associated with this state of mind and becoming more and more an integral part of the completeness of this process of unfoldment, are the imagination and all the finer sensibilities, which *must* be so associated that a delicate state of balance can be preserved.

The child's reason and judgment are not yet awakened. Consequently, we cannot say "he is absorbing all knowledge through intellectual activity, or the consciously directed thought processes," as we are in the habit of seeing them used under the direction of will power and reason.

The Intuition Takes the Place of Reason In Early Childhood

The question naturally arises at this state of our explanation, "Is there any process associated with this activity and receptivity, any state of understanding which may be said to act in place of the reason, which would be selective of values in gathering impressions, through which the individual child may get only those which are most constructive in the unfoldment of his particular individuality?" Most decidedly, yes, the intuition does just this. So long as the child remains in the state of mind where all his impressions come through intuition, we "grown-ups" in association with the child are treading on sacred ground and should learn to protect him most carefully from all interference. The deepest and most lasting impressions of our lives, we all know, come to us during this precious period.

Within the Child Lie All Possibilities

We admit that at no time during our lives is there a period of two or three years, when so much actual knowledge is received and assimilated, as during the period which starts at birth; and yet, into this period comes no activity of consciously directed thought, human reason, or will power. Does it not seem, in the light of so-called education and its multitudinous activities over the world today, from laboratory to classroom, from pre-kindergarten to adult education classes, that it should be worth while for leaders to pause and ponder over this significant fact?

First Three Years of Childhood Proves This Theory

Even the "Wise men of old" were guided to where the young child was, and our greatest Teacher said, "Except ye become as a little child ye can in no wise enter the Kingdom of Heaven", and also, "The Kingdom of Heaven is within". When we are willing to learn of the young child, to study what he has, and how he is unconsciously using it to gain this store of knowledge during the first two or three years of his life, we will begin to see and appreciate the problems of the world of education today in their true light.

From Birth to Adolescence The Important Years

In the last ten years educators in all parts of the world are realizing, as never before, the vital need of liberating the vast energy of the "creative impulse" in the education of every child. *Very few* have as yet awakened to the fact, that to *separate* this activity of the creative impulse from its *entire dependence on the intuitive impressions,* is fatal to ultimate balance and constructive value in any life.

We have given all education via *consciously* directed *intellectual endeavor.* This type of mental activity operates as an obstruction to the natural expression of the creative impulse. Thus comparatively few individuals who follow the higher walks of learning are able to catch glimpses of inspiration, and may only use the creative impulse in *spite* of their intellectual activity, *not because* of it.

Consciously Directed Thought An Obstacle in the Path of True Learning

This manner of administering education, (not the learning it includes), is found to be an obstruction to the natural expression of the creative impulse. We need and desire the knowledge of past centuries for our complete development, but if in its getting we lose the path to unfoldment of individuality and its spontaneous expression and radiation, we pay *too high a price*. In each of us is found the *natural desire* for such individual expression. It is our birthright. Even the successful business man or woman has builded upon ideas and visions which do not come as a result of daily routine. Millions of young people who begin a career with joyous expectation (in the offices of the business world) will be heard from apart from the vast machine which they enter, *only* in proportion as they express *originality* and *initiative*.

Routine Does Not Develop Constructively

In those who seem to be gifted beyond their fellows is discovered the creative impulse functioning in its natural association with some specific trend. Our attention is attracted to them; we call them talented. They may have no greater gift than those who seem to be wholly lacking, only because in them the creative impulse finds no obstruction. Liberate the creative impulse, open the way for its expression, and its association with some specific gift may come in an instant, and thus *everyone* is found to be talented. When the creative impulse is found actively associated with a specific trend it gains momentum and becomes a more positive force. Thus we have seen it operate in many gifted people, though constantly battling with consciously directed thought and its inhibitions. In many cases, to quiet this "monster" who stands in their way, they resort to drugs, etc., which for the *time being* act as an anesthetic to this machine within, and allow, for a short period, these visions to get by and become expressed with spontaneity and charm.

The Creative Impulse When Liberated Becomes An Aid To All Lines of Endeavor

When a person resorts to this type of assistance he is undermining the poise of his individuality and slowly destroying future hope of a greater expression. "Where there is no vision the people perish". This is as true today as it was ages ago.

Vision is the result of the creative impulse in its natural activity, fed by the intuition, formulated, made beautiful, idealized by the imagination, and thus made spontaneously available. All forms of art, whatever the expression, are found to be the result of vision. But only in proportion to the expression of a truth idealized and liberated beyond the realm of the personal, into the realm of the universal, may we hope that the achievement will outlive the passing years. We must also remember that the realm of the universal can never be approached through consciousness of self in any form.

Interests In Spiritual Truths Developed Through Intuition

Thinkers the world over are coming to the realization that when the right principle is used upon which to base education in its unfoldment, there will be found a unity between the spiritual and scientific. What is now being done in all lines of advance proves this point conclusively. Space, time, electrons, laws of gravitation, etc., all theories we have held as true for generations, are fading away before the progress of today's realization.

The artist says, "When I can remain childlike, I get inspiration"; so in the *imitation* of being children, we find the unbalanced tribe of Bohemia today. Einstein says, "Within a few years discoveries will be made chiefly in the spiritual realm", as opposed to the material. He has recently put forth the most advanced theory of the universe in a tiny pamphlet. Dimnet says: "Children are all prophets and seers before the age of ten years"; and also that the thought stream (which he so vividly describes) is prevented in each of us from flowing clearly with a purpose, because of eddies and whirlpools, caused by personal reactions.

The World Needs Individual Development

Will Durant (who has made philosophy popular) admits he has been ushered into a new unknown world by his baby daughter. Prominent business men and financiers often admit that they are guided by what they call their "hunches", *not* by carefully thought out plans. Many times when an individual receives a mental impression or vision of some idea or plan (in a flash—instantaneously, so to speak), he is accepting what the creative impulse brings him via the intuition, which is our practical human way of receiving inspiration. This type of impression has been commonly called "hunches". Educators everywhere are endeavoring to lay aside the mechanization of the individual, which has come through all forms of modern education. To make possible the liberation of the creative impulse (via intuition) is the universal answer to this problem. The young child is a bundle of possibilities in *expression* and *impression;* the expression vocal, the impression intuitive. Within the first two or three years he will gain more actual knowledge than in any other period of the same length during his lifetime, entirely through the medium of intuition.

Intuition the Basis of Individuality

Intellect or reason does not function to any appreciable extent during this period. In all activity he remains unconscious of self. His first awareness of self comes through physical sensation. So long as his impressions come via the intuition his interests are apart from self. His imagination is awakened at this time and becomes the most valuable aid to the creative impulse. The constructive function of the imagination formulates and adjusts the ideas that come via the creative impulse. So long as this association remains intact, all activity of the imagination is bound to be constructive. The creative impulse is the incentive to all activity, physical and mental. During this early time when all knowledge comes via the intuitive impressions, the finer sensibilities are also awakened and nourished.

Child Consciousness Complete In All Desired Characteristics

Thus, the creative impulse, the root of true individuality, is fed and nourished by the intuitive impressions, liberated through the normal functioning of the imagination, thus keeping open the channel for the full and free expression of this impulse now understood to be the sum and substance of individuality and balance. Whenever any nervous reactions result in physical sensation, via tension, we begin to be self-conscious and the crucial point of this change takes place when vocal expression (which is the main avenue of human expression) registers in sensation.

Speech Sounds Depend On Elemental Sounding Board For Resonance

When the back of the skull is understood to be the elemental reflector for all vocal sound, we will be following nature's way to produce vocal sounds, which give the essence of motive power and are the purest of resonance. It is this condition alone upon which the human family have always depended for the natural speech sounds.

In the case of the young child the sound waves

are attracted to this elemental sounding board through the large nerve center at the base of the skull, and are thus naturally brought into relation to the Inter-osseous spaces. Here we find a sound reflector of unlimited capacity and used without physical sensation, which nature has adjusted for this use in each human being. These sounds are made by the young in all nature for their protection, and register no physical sensation whatever in production. They are thus instantly projected into outer space, where their expansion and radiation is unlimited.

When Resonance Is Ample No Physical Sensation In Speech Sounds

We marvel at babies who cry for hours with no sign of hoarseness following. So long as vocal expression comes via pure resonance, we have escaped the first cause of self-consciousness. Consequently, the creative channel is as yet unobstructed.

We find, then, that the first cause of the myriads of ills which follow in the wake of consciousness of self in each human being, mental and physical, may be understood and avoided. Through this analysis we arrive at the logical conclusion that vocal sounds in every child up to the age of two or three years, come naturally on the highest pitches; we can safely say in the octave from high "C" to the "C" above—sounds which most "grown-ups" scarcely hear, much less are able to express with spontaneity and abandon.

Highest Pitches Retained To Keep Speech Sounds Free

This octave from high "C" to the "C" above, contains "The stones the builders have rejected" in all generations. It is the connecting link between natural vocal expression and its elemental reflector. These extreme pitches come as a result of the instantaneous reflection of vocal sound from the elemental sounding board, which is the back of the skull, and is commonly known as the "Inter-osseous" spaces. When vocal sound is the result of this reflection it contains all the carrying power which will ever be needed to fill space adequately—and does so through instantaneous expansion. To our adult ears (that are only seeking adult vocal expression) these sounds are not musical, for they contain only half of the adult musical tone we are accustomed to hear. So long as this vocal expression of the child comes via reflection, there will be no reaction in sensation. He thus may retain in all lines of his growth and development the spontaneity and joy which alone are the result of such expression.

Allow All That Is Within the Child to be Spontaneously Expressed

When this great principle is accepted as fundamental in all education, the pre-school child will be allowed to express vocally in this octave at all times. Only gradually will he add the pitches below without losing this extreme octave, which is the natural connection between vocal vibration and its elemental reflector. As the lower notes are added, they will also come thus via reflection. By the time the age of adolescence is reached, all of their depth and color will also gradually be added via reflection. Mature vocal expression will arrive with a perfect evenly tuned scale of not less than three octaves of musical tones, as spontaneous in expression as the bird's song, because physical sensation has never in any way been found necessary to be associated with this production of vocal sound. Thus, from the vocal standpoint, many years of nerve-racking, so-called vocal study and practice and millions of dollars will be saved. Thousands of disappointed young souls who fail in becoming "great singers" would find their expression in other avenues, while universal singing would be the spontaneous expression of joy nature intended for each of us.

Individuality Should Be Developed In Every Child Through Education

From the standpoint of education and the unfoldment of individuality, when vocal expression is thus kept apart and free from conscious physical sensation, the way is kept open for the activity of the creative impulse, and we find it not only possible, but the most logical means of allowing the child as he develops, to recognize that he is at all times depending on his intuitive impressions and their spontaneous *expression* for the unfoldment of his true individuality via his education. Through this adjustment, his intellect becomes his servant, the reason and judgment walk hand in hand to follow his bidding. His creative impulse remains the incentive for all activity and his imagination grows apace and functions only constructively, as it formulates and adjusts all that his creative impulses bring him. His thinking is clear and unobstructed by reactions which come via consciousness of self. (For no self-consciousness can operate so long as physical sensation does not obstruct vocal expression.)

The Imagination of Value Only When Used Constructively

The intuition and imagination have been kept in the association of the negative and destructive forces for so long a time, through the influence of "isms and osophies" and in the physical realm, that the trend of education has not yet been an aid to their legitimate growth and to the recognition of their association with the best and highest tendencies of mankind. It is only through the separation of mental and physical activity from reactions in sensation, (resulting from conscious direction of will power), that we may see and recognize the unlimited power they possess. When we can understand the way by which this may be accomplished, and when all consciousness of self is thus found to be unnecessary in any avenue of unfoldment, shall we be able to allow the intuition and imagination to take their *rightful* place in the science of education. Their power lies only in their association with liberated, constructive, affirmative thinking, the incentive of which is found to be the creative impulse.

Value of Intuition But Little Understood

When the *imagination* is normally functioning, its activity in *every* nature is associated with and invigorates that of the *finer sensibilities,* as well. The joy of living each day in true spontaneous expression, will bring all the thrills youth is seeking, in a balanced way which unfolds true individuality. An interest in the realm beyond the physical and mental is a logical result of this manner of unfoldment, through which *balance is attained* and *individuality becomes outstanding.*

Use of Will Power Leads to Self-Consciousness and Is the First Wrong Step

Most problems which confront the social worker, in his struggle to uplift and develop the masses, are the logical result of ignorance and misunderstanding of the natural equipment of every normal child at birth. It is *now possible* to gain a vision of these early years, which allows an entire adjustment and balance of each child to the world about him, through the liberation of the creative impulse via the channel intended thus to unfold his entire nature. The first twelve years of his life should be understood as having formed a basic condition, upon which the years of maturity may safely be builded. When parents and teachers gain this vision they will adequately value this fundamental equipment, and cherish and protect it accordingly.

Difficulties Overcome Only Through Parents and Teachers

In order to adjust this plan to our educational processes, there need be no expenditure for change in curriculum, apparatus or equipment. This adjustment will take place when parents and teachers are able to understand and require that the child be allowed to remain in the "child consciousness", from which basis he will naturally unfold. Intuitive in all his impressions, the child will be constructive and affirmative in his thinking, and will express his true selfhood with confidence, apart from reactions in physical sensation; having throughout his unfoldment spontaneous activity of mind and body which fosters sincerity of purpose and constructive imagination, apart from self.

We have just described some of the characteristics of the unspoiled child-consciousness, which will remain untouched by time and growth into full maturity, when *this* vision is applied with understanding to the first twelve years of his life. It is the "ounce of prevention" which allows each life to attain ultimate balance and individuality.

Education Must Begin With Parents and Teachers

It may be true that humanity will first have to recognize the value of this vision through its adaptation to the needs of those who have reached maturity, and are found unhappy and dissatisfied with life and themselves—resulting from years of repression of latent powers within them, since for them the creative impulse has not been liberated through nature's plan. But it is most encouraging to know that at *any age* one may apply this vision as the "pound of cure" and thus may gain the realization of true individuality and its spontaneous expression, through the application of a few fundamental principles to his daily experience.

Adult Problems Settled By This Understanding

To adjust the application of these principles to the needs of maturity, we must first release the body from sensation in activity, which liberates the main nerve centers from the sensation of muscular action. Thus each set of muscles becomes independently active, without reactions in sensation—thus minimizing waste of energy and fatigue.

Second, Unified Diction (Speech Analysis). This form of diction specifically applies the same plan to the activity of speech organs, liberating them from sensation and fatigue, and correcting also most forms of speech impediment or limitation.

Third, Constructive Voice Production. A manner of building vocal tone which depends entirely upon resonance.

Every Normal Person Has All Essentials of Musical Voice

When the whole body, including the speech organs, is thus released for all activity, the speech sound gradually brings a reflection of sound waves from the entire structure of skull and body which results in an abundance of resonance (without physical sensation). Correct singing thus becomes "Vocalized Speech".

When our main medium of human expression (the voice) is thus equipped with an abundance of resonance, *at all times available* without conscious direction or sensation, we discover *an escape from self-consciousness* in all expression, through which medium we are *again* established in the "child-consciousness". We may experience the activity of the liberated creative impulse, intuitive impressions, constructive imagination, spontaneous activity of mind and body, used with a *minimum* of sensation and fatigue, since we now find *no consciousness of self* resulting from nervous reaction in sensation.

Note: "The First Twelve Years" in pamphlet form, copyright 1930 by M. Barbereux-Parry.

IV

THE CHILD VOICE

The question is often asked, "At what age should a child begin to take singing lessons?" In the old way of working with the voice, it has seemed a question that has had to be answered through the example of individual cases. If a child of ten, or twelve, or fourteen seemed to have a voice of promise, in some cases vocal training at this age has seemed to work out satisfactorily. The opinion of teachers varies on this as upon most other points in the development of the voice, but to answer the question intelligently from the standpoint of *this theory*, one must know much about the voice and its analysis in order to be able to judge for himself.

To begin with the voices of little folk of two years of age, we find every little child is at home in his vocal expression in the octave between high "C" and the "C" above. These pitches are the natural expression of the young child, but in no way can the sounds the little people make upon these pitches be called singing, for when the *adult* is considering a singing tone, his ear is seeking what can only be found in the adult voice—the blending of the two qualities which permit the tone to have ample resonance.

When vocal tone has ample resonance it flows, and the legato and sostenuto which are the background of beautiful singing are the natural result of this blending of the two qualities (or the two sets of overtones). In the voice of the young child, only the upper quality (or upper set of overtones)—the *carrying power,* is in evidence. This upper quality in its most extreme condition is thin, piercing shrillness, and has been given to the young by nature for their protection. When little children sing on the pitches within this extreme octave, the sounds they make are much more like the chirping of birds and in no way express sustained effects. These sounds allow the child to call playmates at long distances, and make possible the rapid, spontaneous use of the speech organs, for the carrying power that is embodied in the child voice at this age is all the carrying power (in embryo) that the mature voice will ever need.

Because of this, we should most carefully cherish these very characteristics of freedom and spontaneity, in order that as the child goes on to the age of adolescence, nature will bring to him in every possible way *all* the motive power which lies within this upper quality, freely reflected and gradually distributed through a compass of three octaves and over. Unfortunately, the world has been ignorant of this wonderful plan of nature to furnish the individual, in the first twelve or thirteen years of his life, with sufficient motive power to be used through all his mature years in all forms of vocal expression.

We have also, *unfortunately,* used our adult measurements in relationship to good vocal tone for the *child voice as well,* and in so doing, have completely *lost sight of the marvelous possibilities* of the child voice *when allowed to remain* in its *natural* condition to the age of adolescence.

In the singing of children, we should at *no time* listen for legato or sostenuto. We should at no time listen for *depth, breadth,* or *color. These* belong to the *adult* vocal realm. Within the realm of the child voice we should look only for freedom, spontaneity, clearness and carrying power, and in so doing allow nature's great plan to come to its fullest development. At the age of adolescence, when we say the child voices are changing, (if *this* plan were carried out) this change in no way would be *noticeable,* or in *no way* would the child be *conscious* of its taking place; for when this carrying power (the upper overtones) has been allowed to increase in its own way up to the age of adolescence, with no conscious direction, and no thought of its being made as a singing tone, we would find nature ready to add gradually the low overtones which embody the color, depth, richness and musical sweetness which we are seeking, and *nature's way* of doing this is so *gradual* that the child himself can never become aware of the change.

All of the difficulties in children's voices and *all forms of speech impediment,* (during and previous to the age of adolescence,) can be *directly* traced to the *misunderstanding* of the child voice and to its misdirection during the years *preceding adolescence.* Not only in the singing voice, but in the speech as well, can we trace the deadly influence of this neglect. When a child's voice remains in the realm of upper overtones (the child quality) his speech organs have spontaneous and independent action, for the extreme state of carrying power which *belongs* to the *natural* child voice, is given in order that the speech organs may also do their work spontaneously, without conscious direction; thus *preventing and eliminating all forms of defective speech.*

Up to the present time, the child's voice has been encouraged to leave its natural realm of upper overtones and their spontaneous and unlimited carrying power, for from the time he enters pre-kindergarten, it is expected that he shall sing in the compass where the average adult voice finds singing easy (around middle "C" and the octave above). This misplacement of the child's vocal condition results in his endeavoring to imitate, the best he can, the sounds made by adult voices in a compass where little, if *any,* natural resonance comes into *his tone;* and eventually he becomes more conscious of the speech organs as vocal sounds become more difficult in production. Thus he loses all spontaneity and joy of producing vocal sounds, in both speaking and singing. His spontaneity grows less and less and, in all cases where a child suffers from defective speech, the trouble can be clearly traced to nervous contraction in some form entirely due to his lack of natural resonance, which has been lost through separating him from his own realm of vocal sounds.

All difficulties found with children's voices during the *age of adolescence, can be traced to this same cause,* that of *low* overtones coming in as they do in abundance, *with no possible chance* to blend with the *carrying power* nature has furnished through *upper* overtones from early babyhood, but which through our *ignorance* of their ultimate value, we have *misplaced or entirely obliterated.*

When children's voices are allowed to remain throughout all the years *preceding adolescence* in this realm of thin, clear sounds with their wealth of motive power, and nature is *allowed to proceed with her plan* uninterruptedly, ninety-five children out of every hundred would go from the eighth grade into high school with not less than two octaves of perfectly tuned musical tones which they use with no *consciousness of production* whatever, no thought of *breath or its adjustment,* and with a joy in singing which they would carry through all the years of their lives. The mental and vocal condition which we would find as a result of this understanding would make it possible, for those who cared to follow it as a profession, to eliminate three or four years of private lessons in the studio, which are *now* spent in so-called "voice placement and development", *made necessary only* by the misunderstanding of the child voice before the time of adolescence.

In order that vocal tone may become professionally valuable, it must be so produced that with it the singer may fill large spaces. The *carrying power* which *this* condition necessitates must be based upon the development of *either* breath or resonance capacity and control. The fact can be proven by those who have spent years in vocal study and analysis, that these two factors *in no way* can be combined with *truly constructive* results. To *understand* the adult voice and its possibilities through *this analysis* of the child voice, so clearly shows that in all we do with the adult voice we are only applying what the old adage says is the "pound of cure"; while, if *nature's plans* for the vocal condition were *allowed* to come to their *fulfillment* through *this* understanding of the child voice and its adjustment, we can readily see that all these questions of voice building would be much more the result of the application of the "ounce of prevention" which, the old adage says, "is better than the pound of cure".

V

ACTIVITY

The term "activity" in its everyday significance, associated with educational unfoldment, is usually separated into two general classes—mental and physical. The mental is again subdivided into the spiritual and intellectual, and the physical may also be subdivided into the nervous and muscular.

When we consider physical activity we concede that muscular activity is the result of a mental stimulus through the medium of the nerves. For our purpose, this recognition is illuminating. Mental activity in its adaptation to our analysis recognizes intellectual activity as being the medium for all uses of education, and the development of education as it is understood today is recognized as wholly dependent upon intellectual activity.

From early childhood (at least to the time the child has reached the age of two years), grown-ups in their association with him, begin to be interested in awakening intellectual activity. In some cases there seems to be retained, throughout the years of intellectual growth, a balance which is much to be desired between so-called intellectual and physical activity and that of the finer sensibilitites, which brings the individual in adult years to a state of poise which is to be desired; the results of which are shown not only in the every-day pursuits, but in the general disposition as well. It is to be regretted, however, that it is the exceptional case which thus arrives at maturity with a balanced mind and body.

In the process of development which follows the early recognition and stimulation of the intellect, in the majority of cases, we find from year to year a sense of growing disproportion throughout the entire nature. This leads to a state of inhibited nervous impulses, and a gradual dulling of the finer sensibilities, while as the years go on the consciousness of the individual seems to become more chaotic, and a constant warfare ensues between opposing forces within. Because of this, only two ways are found to evade the results of this seeming state of unbalance—one being a constant feeling of suppression through the mental and physical via the domination of the will power; the other being the concentration of all the forces within, and their expression through some individual channel of talent or creative feeling, resulting in a state of mind in which nearly all artists are found to be involved.

Scarcely ever do we find an *artist in any line,* the free expression of whose talent has not in some way disturbed or distorted the true harmony of his entire nature. The self-consciousness which is the result of thought propelled by will power (which we call intellectual activity), operates *always in opposition* to the spontaneous expression of intuitive impressions, and will constantly annihilate all that comes by way of inspiration and creative feeling.

When every individual, through his educational unfoldment, is given the understanding by which all knowledge may come to him through intuitive impressions, *instead of* consciously directed thought, in *no way* is his unfoldment *ever* obstructed by the consciousness of self. Thus his thought naturally is liberated, and the forces of his whole nature coordinate and cooperate during the process of unfoldment so harmoniously, that *education* becomes the *medium* through which *creative feeling* and *inspiration* are blended. This allows *each nature* to *find* the way through which all knowledge and culture may come to him *so blended* with creative feeling and talent during its unfoldment, that as a result artistic natures reach their complete expression and perfect poise, and every individual will be found to possess, in some measure at least, a talent and its logical unfoldment. Such a state of understanding allows all of the finer sensibilities in each individual their spontaneous expression and radiation.

VI

ANALYSIS OF RELEASE

This analysis of the human body and its activity is based upon the realization that *any* and *all* physical activity may become *sensationless* when released from conscious mental direction and control (will power). All other systems of physical development have been carried out entirely through the application of conscious mental direction.

Take for instance, the act of so-called deep breathing. The lungs are situated on either side of the spinal column, in the back. The base of the lungs is found at the waist line, extending therefrom upward underneath the shoulder blades. The consideration of lung expansion has always been taken through the action of the chest muscles; chest expansion being used as a basis of measurement (at the top of the body), and the expansion of the diaphragm as a measurement at the waist line. With this understanding, in order to fill the lungs one is supposed to expand them outward and upward to their fullest extent; and the more muscular action used in the region of the diaphragm, and even as far as the abdominal muscles, the deeper the breathing accomplished.

The truth of the matter is that from a simple anatomical viewpoint, *this* theory of deep breathing, although it has been accepted for so long, has *no basis in fact.* When the diaphragmatic muscles are distended, in proportion as they are consciously held outward, the *base* of the lungs is as consciously compressed by the action. In other words, when we do so-called diaphragmatic breathing, *instead* of filling the lungs from their base (which lies at the waist line in the back), the muscular action of the diaphragm is pulling against and compressing the lower lobes of the lungs, and consequently *only* the top of the lungs is well filled. When we allow the body to droop over the waist line in front with a feeling of caving in at the pit of the stomach, we are in reality *releasing the base* of the lungs and giving them the freedom which allows them to fill deeply. This sort of deep breathing gives a feeling of an expansion of the back just above the waist line on either side, and from thence gradually filling the upper lobes; and by so doing the lungs are completely filled, *without* the muscular tension which always makes us feel that to leave the air in the lungs requires a muscular holding.

This type of activity gives the feeling that the *chest is filled last of all* with only a slight sense of expansion. To explain: a high chest, which is supposed to result from proper breathing, is usually a chest which is consciously held up by the muscles, and may or may not denote lung capacity underneath. When the chest is properly expanded through *natural* breathing, it appears from the outside at all times to be fully developed, with no hollow between the shoulder blades. This posture never results in any conscious muscular holding. This activity of the lungs allows the shoulder blades always to hang loosely, never to be thrown back, until the line of the shoulder blades is in no way visible because of the *filled-in space* between them.

When we are considering released activity of the body, we find it is liberated from conscious will power direction and sensation. We must next analyze the spinal column. The spinal column is composed of a loosely adjusted set of vertebrae, each one sitting within the one below like a pile of teacups. These vertebrae are held together by a loosely woven set of cartilages which extend from one end to the other of the spine. We have always been taught that a *lateral* curvature of the spine denotes a most abnormal condition, and hasten to remedy it with every possible appliance and exercise.

Wherever a curvature in the spine exists, the vertebrae are found to be sitting so closely together that the nerve centers which are within each vertebra are without food; incapable of circulation, for it is through the circulation that the nerve centers are fed. As long as the vertebrae sit lightly one within the other, and *movement in all directions* remains free and released, we know that the circulation is carrying food to the nerve centers and their functioning is normal. The moment there is any obstruction to this carrying of food to the nerve centers through circulation, some part of our body will soon be crying loudly for help, for we know all parts of the body are directed from nerve centers which lie within the spinal column.

Isn't it queer that with all this understanding of the danger of a *lateral* curvature it has never been brought to our notice that an inward or outward curvature has the same results in the restriction of food supply of the nerve centers? It is rarely that we find an adult whose spinal column does not bend outward over the shoulder blades and inward at the waist line, and outward over the hips; and all these people suffer more or less with various forms of nervous fatigue, and put the blame for it in any and all places except that of spinal curves. The *old idea* that to be *erect* we must throw the shoulders back and breathe deeply through the expansion of the diaphragmatic muscles, does give a fine appearance in front and develops high chest through the application of muscular control; but look on that picture and then upon this! The poor spinal column that is doing its best to support the whole body, the weight of which is thrown upon it from the shoulder blades and the diaphragm, is curved inward and outward in a truly horrifying way when we know the results of this curvature, which cannot be evaded.

It is true that in recent years these conditions have been improved through the application of osteopathy and kindred forms of treatment, wherein the patient is laid upon the table, and gradually through manipulation the poor vertebrae are pulled apart and a normal circulation throughout the nerve centers is allowed to take place. *As long as* the patient remains upon the table, it is possible for this circulation to go on, but the moment he stands up and walks off again, the weight and the strain of the body is thrown upon the spine with the same result as before.

The only possible way to adjust a condition which allows the spinal column to become more and more normal, is to give it the *support of the muscles* which extend on either side of the back from the shoulders to the hips (the corners of the back); thus a muscular pillar is formed on either side of the spine which gradually takes the support of the whole body *from the spine* and allows it to resume its natural plasticity.

The caved-in position of the body at the pit of the stomach, which has been alluded to above, eliminates the curve at the waist line in the back, although it does seem to shorten the length of the waist in front. The drooping of the shoulders which is advocated in this type of release, does appear to allow the chest muscles to become depressed, and rounded shoulders with hollow chest is the first appearance of this type of release; but, while we are liberating the spinal column and building the corners of the back to remove the strain from the spine, we must use the released activity which gradually builds and adjusts a muscular condition that becomes naturally structural in the support of a high chest, breadth of body under the arms, filling in between the shoulder blades, and the lifting of the chin which releases the muscular tension from the back of the neck, liberating the large nerve center at the base of the brain. This position also prevents the enlargement of the front of the neck which is called the double chin.

For the sake of analysis we will go back to the old condition of a high chest muscularly held, protruding diaphragm and abdomen in a constant state of tension, with the spinal column curving out over the shoulders, in at the waist line and out over the hips, resulting in a state of tension across the back of the neck (which we find habitual in almost all adults). Added to this, a hollow between the shoulder blades in the back and a protruding collar bone on either side in front.

In reversing all these conditions, first of all to liberate the spinal column to its normal state of plasticity and *uncurved line,* it is necessary to liberate certain nerve centers in the body from a triangle of tension. This triangle of tension is liberated first through the caving in of the pit of the stomach, which liberates the Solar Plexus from the clutch of the diaphragm—the first point of the triangle; we liberate the nerve center at the back of the neck through lifting the chin—the second point of the triangle; we liberate the sciatic nerve in each hip through the release of the hip joints, using the same position as in sitting—the third point of the triangle. To bring the body into the state of poise through which it remains free from this triangle of tension, we must use the proper muscular movements which we call releases, with the application of liberated thought until the *correct state* of muscular support is achieved, upon which it all depends. In the ideals of the old Greeks, we find *this type* of body exemplified to a most satisfying degree.

Four of the best known examples are the Winged Victory, Venus de Milo, Apollo Belvedere and Mercury. We observe the inclined plane of the spinal column, the developed pillars on each side which serve as the support (a corner on each side of the back). The depressed line at the diaphragm, the plastic bend of the hip joint, the freedom of the knee and ankle, which proves to us conclusively that when the physical body is so released it reaches its highest state of perfection, in repose as well as activity.

VII

RELEASED ACTIVITY

The Barbereux System of Activity Release approaches the study and analysis of the human body and its activity with an entirely *new vision* and its *universal* application. What humanity seems most in need of in all forms of education and unfoldment today, is a vision of human needs and their fulfillment which is based on the universal.

At this time, the world has been awakened to a new understanding of human beings in their relationship to each other, because of the close proximity which has been established throughout the world through the adaptation of speech and vocal expression to the radio. Because of this fact, there is a greater need of a fundamental and universal understanding of speech and vocal sound, and their entire dependence one upon the other, than has been known before.

We believe that the *Barbereux System* meets this need. It is generally admitted by those in a position to know world conditions, that all forms of education used up to the present time have been found deplorably lacking when we come to the point of realizing that it is *unfoldment* which the individual should have, *through the adjustment to education,* (and not accretion and mechanization). Unfoldment cannot take place until the individual has been *liberated from himself.* The primal source of unfoldment is spontaneity, and spontaneity is lost by the individual the moment he begins to be mechanized, mentally or physically. In order to reverse and lay aside this state of mental and physical mechanism, which has become universal, a new vision of liberation is gained through what is called *Activity Release,* which may be applied to the human body at *any age.*

The analysis and understanding of the body, which has been given to us through the science of anatomy, we use to make clear the application and understanding of *Released Activity.* All mental and physical activity has been operated *between* the two points of *force* and *resistance,* through the universal application of will power. As long as the human being is *dependent* upon will power for motivation, he is *imprisoned* between force and resistance, and fifty percent of the nervous energy used is wasted. This drive of will power has caused us to misunderstand and misuse many important forms of physical action. The *most important* of these is the act of breathing. When the action of the body is understood through application of *Released Activity,* the act of breathing is found to be based upon the law of vacuum, and is *wholly adequate* when used with this understanding. We have been taught that the anatomical reason for breathing is to supply oxygen to the blood, between the heart beats (the basis of circulation). When all forms of physical action are found to be sensationless, the intake and outgo of the breath in the lungs is so slight that our attention is not called in any way to the muscular act of breathing. This point of understanding enables the Solar Plexus (which is known to be the nerve center from which *all sensation* in the body is derived), *to escape* from ten percent of the tension of all physical action. In other words, to drive the act of deep breathing through the force of will power keeps the Solar Plexus in a state of constant tension from which the whole body has no escape.

As soon as one is able to prove to himself the fallacy of so-called deep breathing, he is ready and able to make and understand the analysis of the body and its activity from an entirely new viewpoint. When one is able to lay aside his *dependence* upon what has been called deep breathing, it is readily seen that one of the most active and strongest muscles in the body (the diaphragm) can be disassociated in its activity from the clutch it has held about the Solar Plexus; which conclusively proves this action to be the greatest source of tension and sensation throughout the body. To this extreme activity of the diaphragm can be traced an entirely wrong usage of the whole body, and a state of posture which must be entirely changed.

The basis of this posture is found to be a triangle of tension which lies between the sciatic nerve in each hip, the Solar Plexus, and the nerve center at the upper end of the spine at the base of the brain.

Upon this triangle rests the support of the body in such a manner as to throw the hips and abdomen forward. This posture makes it very difficult to adjust the chest, shoulders and back to a normal position. The most important problem in adjusting the whole body to a state of perfect poise and balance, which is necessary to give independent activity to each set of muscles, is to find a muscular condition which gives the body a perfect state of support, the use of which *does not* throw strain and tension on any nerve center.

The *Barbereux System* proves there is a muscular state of support which exists between the shoulders and the hip joints on either side of the back—the corners of the back they may be called. When the action of these muscles is *understood* and *liberated* from *this viewpoint,* we find a perfect state of posture to be the result—each set of muscles in the body independent in activity. The reaction of one set of muscles, one upon the other, through tension, is entirely laid aside.

These pillars of support on the corners of the back liberate and protect the whole spinal column from end to end in its activity; the movement of each vertebra, one within the other, so free and plastic that the circulation is entirely liberated throughout the whole body. Instead of posture which we are accustomed to see, of the rounding out of the back over the shoulder blades, in at waist line, out over the hips, with flat chest and drooping shoulders, protruding stomach and abdomen, we find the back to become a slightly inclined plane from back of the neck to the base of the hips, with flattened shoulder blades filled in between, the fully filled in chest, graceful curves at the waist line, and a stomach and abdomen which *does not protrude.*

It is most interesting and convincing to find the exemplification of this type of poise and posture to have been demonstrated in the Greek art centuries ago—as in the Venus de Milo, the Apollo Belvedere, and many other examples of the perfection of Grecian sculpture.

Through the application of *Released Activity* to the human body over a period of two years at least, the complete change of posture and entire readjustment of action and reaction of the whole body is almost unbelievable. In actual weight, proportion, line and measurement, the body is found to have regained a state of youth.

The triangle of tension (previously explained), is laid aside. Each set of muscles in the body regains an independence of movement which has not been experienced since early childhood. The head and neck are found independent in their activity also; and the movement of the arms in their sockets, and the release of the hip, knee and ankle joints give a spontaneity and grace of line and poise, the results of which are entirely new and convincing.

This plan of activity is entirely basic, and is not gained through will power drive, repetition and drill. Ten minutes of time devoted to these movements twice a day keeps the whole body in a perfect condition, and no other time devoted to exercise is needed, for when the body has attained this new adjustment, this small amount of time is *enough* to *retain* its freedom and *protect* it from the old, everyday routine of movement. The *outdoor* amusements which have before been considered *essential* to the well being of the body, such as tennis, golf, horseback riding, dancing, etc., are *now* indulged in for the pure joy of doing—not because they are needed.

Students of the *Barbereux System* can in no way expect to gain adequate and ultimate results in any department of the work until they have established these principles and adjusted and adapted them to their daily needs.

VIII

CONCENTRATION

In all forms of mental endeavor, great respect has been given to the power of concentration. In many centers of learning special courses are offered which are said to develop this ability to the highest degree. The power of concentration is supposed to give one the understanding and analysis of his thought processes to such an extent that he is able to focus all his mental equipment upon the subjects in hand, and at the same time to shut out from his thought all attention and interest in everything outside himself.

This accepted form of education has constantly given to the world the association of all mental and intellectual attainments through the application of consciously directed thought, motivated by the will power. This manner of approach is so universal and has been accepted without question for so many centuries, that to step aside and consider any other manner of procedure in the unfoldment of the individual, appears almost heresy. In spite of this accepted scholastic thought, there is rapidly growing in all parts of the world among intelligent people, the realization that in many and most important factors, this form of scholasticism and dependence upon will power, which we have so firmly believed in, has woefully failed to assist in the progress of individuals and their ability to meet successfully life's problems in a practical, constructive way.

A new educational movement which is being agitated widely undertakes to prove that each one of us comes into the world endowed with all the potentialities necessary to the well-rounded adult, and that the greatest need of education today is to find the most effective means of so unfolding and directing these potentialities that we will be shown the way through which every individual may attain a perfect balance, thus associating his life with all that is creative, inspirational and ideal in his world.

For the sake of argument, we must for the time being at least accept the theory that to direct thought consciously is our first and greatest obstacle. Consciously directed thought and will power stand at the portal where the creative impulse and intuitive impressions would enter in, and say, "Thus far and no farther". In other words, we must realize that to awaken and unfold the creative impulse, which is the beginning of the true individuality in each one of us, we must make use of intuitive impressions which we always find are given abundantly to those who are supposed to have what is called the artistic temperament.

Is it not strange that each human footstep which has been found to be epoch making in the progress of the world, can be traced to the potency of inspiration, whether it be in the fields of scientific invention or in the following of an ideal in the arts? This being true, it is almost unbelievable that we have *never yet* approached in any practical way the unfoldment of the individual through the *liberation* of the *creative impulse* and *intuitive impressions*. With this new vision of unfoldment, we may go back to the point of concentration. To learn to concentrate the thought and lay aside *outside* interference requires considerable study and application. But learning to concentrate through the separation of the thought from the interference of the *five physical senses* and *their* reactions, goes much more deeply into the mental side of the question, and proves to each individual how much he has become limited and imprisoned through dependence upon conscious direction and will power.

The first step in the direction of our thought forces in their adjustment toward logical unfoldment, is that of absorbing interest. For instance, to be wholly absorbing, the interest must include the imagination. We often notice children playing "make believe", and in so doing, we find their power of concentration to be much greater than anything adults can accomplish in that line. We also find it *becomes* so through the power of imagination, associated *with* this interest. To illustrate: making a rocking chair become a real engine in the thought of the child is in direct proportion to the amount of imagination applied, and its application is made through the child's intense desire to direct the engine.

It is often said that the best creative work accomplished by anyone at any time is done at the point of desperation. In the case of adults, desperation may be the excuse, or the result of the most intense degree of desire, which is found to be the impelling force—the imagination expressing the creative and the interest supplying the incentive. This combination of desire, imagination and absorbing interest is found in all creative work.

To return to our analysis of the creative impulse, which must be kept free from all reactions of the five physical senses, we must analyze the correlation of three of the five physical senses in their influence, and in so doing we find the *inter*dependence of sight, hearing and feeling quite surprising. In the observation and analysis of the *vocal tone* and its production, for instance, are found forces which are entirely elemental in and through the gamut of human unfoldment. It is because the vocal tone itself is the universal, most important and most fundamental means of human expression and communication. Any factor which can instantaneously bridge the distance between the prehistoric caveman and the well-born child of today, must be accepted as being fundamental and elemental. As in the use of vocal sound, in both cases it most eloquently expresses the deepest human feelings and consequently, since it comes from the seat of our innermost human feelings, its reactions are found to be most illuminating in our search for the release of individual creative expression in its adaptation to educational unfoldment.

When we are making use of the expression of the

vocal tone as fundamental in educational unfoldment, we find it to be the greatest possible assistance in the adjustment of creative thinking (apart from self); for to produce vocal sound and simultaneously to hear that sound during its production, is from our earliest childhood so closely intertwined in our consciousness as to seem impossible to disassociate. Our thought is instantly attracted and held by whatever, for the time being, engages our most intense interest. The more impersonal the interest, the greater the detachment from our personal feelings (self) or their reactions. This detachment of reactions from self is one of the most important factors in concentration and clear thinking, for the five physical senses have limited the activity of our thought forces by their action and reaction to a far greater degree than one would believe possible. We will take, for example, the case of one who does public work in speaking, reading or singing. A point of great importance is to express ideas in either case so vividly that the thought and feelings of the author or composer will be conveyed according to the intention of the one who delivers the message.

If, first of all, the vocal sound in its production is so entirely produced through pure resonance that no physical reactions take place in sensation, the most important *detachment* from self has been accomplished. If, at the same time, the imagination has been so awakened that all of the physical senses run the gamut of emotional expression, we then have a mental and vocal state with which the most vivid pictoral effects can be drawn.

The interest must be kept so apart from self that the *outer* ear (the *physical* hearing) for the time being seems detached, and in no way does the outer hearing associate itself with the results. As long as we remain conscious through our outer hearing of any effects vocally produced, we will not be able to allow vocal sounds their fullest expansion and radiation. The constant association of cause and effect and our *simultaneous* interest in them has been so upheld throughout all present modes of education, that it is most of all responsible for this, the greatest obstacle in all lines of individual unfoldment—self-consciousness. As long as our thought forces are involved with these two extremes simultaneously, we will fail in being able to use true spontaneity in any line of expression.

To be able to concentrate at any time and for any purpose, we must first of all master the understanding of disassociating our thought from the reaction of any or all of the five physical senses, for it is only through *their* interference we find our greatest difficulty.

When the young child is using his most spontaneous expression long before he has become conscious of self, we find this expression uses only the extreme high pitches which belong to the natural child voice. These vocal sounds are the result of pure resonance and entire spontaneity, and *because* of this, result in no physical sensation. These sounds as yet are entirely disassociated from the use of mental direction. When *this* spontaneity of vocal expression is *retained* from earliest childhood to adult age, we will find that the individual by this means has been kept free from self-consciousness in all its forms; and as long as one remains unlimited by thought of self through this spontaneity of vocal expression, it is possible for the individual to gain his knowledge of the world about him *entirely* through *intuitive impressions. These,* in turn, liberate the creative impulse and all that is original, affirmative and constructive throughout his entire unfoldment, in contradiction to the destructive, subjective, and negative forces which are found to be the result of our present mode of scholastic education (to which we have been so long accustomed), and which come through the use of conscious mental direction and will power, resulting in all the forms of self-consciousness, suppression and inhibitions which educators find are most appalling in the youth of today.

IX

SPONTANEITY

In the development of a tonal capacity and compass of three octaves in any voice, we are establishing an unlimited condition for the reflection of sound-waves, the type that is found in the family of stringed instruments. It is possible to develop this capacity in any and every voice, primarily through the ability to use the elemental vocal condition which we find in the young child, the young child who is able to scream and laugh and cry all day long and often all night long, with no ill effects. Going back to the child's capacity, we are in reality finding the way through which every sound of the human voice comes naturally, without sensation. This reflection of sound waves belongs to early childhood and does not bring sensation to the throat, the larynx, the pharynx or the frontal or mouth cavities in their production; and in *no* way do they need the consciousness of breath applied. They are the result of the liberated sets of sound-waves being naturally reflected, first of all from the elemental sounding board (which the child condition of production uses), and are as free from conscious direction as his eyesight or his hearing.

One of the great mistakes which has been made

in association with the vocal condition is that we grownups, as rapidly as possible in all ways, have taken the child away from this condition of spontaneity, and through imitation and direction have given him the feeling that only the vocal sounds made *by adults* were worth while. To go back to the great importance of the establishment of an extreme compass, we find that in the family of stringed instruments tonal value of color and quality as well as power is a direct result of the use of overtones; and in proportion to the free vibration of the whole length of the string, do we get the added vibrations of the segments or partials which are overtones. If the free vibration of the whole string is not fully reflected, the vibration of the segments and the partials is also limited. In other words, when we are seeking the greatest beauty of quality and color in a tone, we find it to have been reflected from the whole sounding-board of the instrument. A pianissimo tone is not beautiful merely because it is a tiny sound or because of restriction or suppression, but because within that delicacy of touch which brings perfect vibration and reflection, is also found the fullest capacity for all the overtones belonging to it; we are also using the full capacity of the sounding board in as perfect proportion as a fortissimo requires, and all the color that could come into a fortissimo is found in the pianissimo in as perfect proportion, only in a lesser quantity.

This, then, is the most important reason for basing the unfoldment of the human voice upon the natural spontaneous condition of the child voice and for developing it from that point, which in a perfectly natural way is a logical unfoldment; and to every adult voice it adds an octave and more of legitimate sounds which, when fully reflected, become perfectly tuned musical tones entirely spontaneous and sensationless in their production.

X

PHONETICS

The subject of phonetics in theory and practice logically follows the trend of all human educational endeavor today. It is based upon a belief of carefully training the human intellect, through the use of will power, drill and conscious repetition, to recognize and accept certain facts and their adaptation to the needs of speech, ear training and vocal expression of all kinds. When a student has thoroughly mastered this form of understanding he is expected to use his voice in all speech expression with a certain refinement of pronunciation, enunciation, diction, shading, inflection and nuance which is found entirely adequate to fill any need of speech expression adapted to all the demands of his art.

When the subject of phonetics is approached from the basic idea of spontaneity and *released activity, intuitively directed,* the student is led to discover and *accept* a vision of his natural ability, which unfolds into a clear and practical recognition of the unlimited capacity of speech expression adaptable to all his needs *without* the use of will power, drill or conscious repetition: a *new vision* of phonetics.

His voice must first become tuned for two octaves at least. This process is accomplished through the awakening and blending of the two sets of overtones, exactly as we proceed to tune any stringed instrument. These two sets of overtones are found in every normal voice, seldom in perfect tune. All the great singers of the world have had this tuning naturally adjusted. This tuning process awakens and unfolds all the latent capacity of the inner ear (intuitive hearing), which results in a perfect expression of pure resonance on every tone. This pure resonance at the same time liberates the speech organs to independent activity in which there is found no resistance, mental or physical. This independent activity of speech organs has not before been found possible to use, since all vocal expression has always depended on some form of breath and its conscious control.

In this approach to all vocal expression, pure resonance is abundantly supplied to each sound expressed, through reflection, expansion and radiation into space. *All dependence on breath is laid aside as our greatest vocal limitation.* The use of pure resonance instead of breath, brings with it an unlimited capacity of *adjustment* and co-ordination of speech and vocal sounds. This results in all production being *apart* from physical sensation. Through the use of pure resonance we find vocal clarity, power, delicacy, shading, inflection and nuance, apart from the need of will power, repetition and drill, and spontaneously adapted to every need of one who speaks, reads or sings. All this proves conclusively that vocal expression belongs in the realm of the mental.

XI

SIMPLICITY

The sum of all vocal training should bring the following result: When any voice has been developed through vocal study, it should come to the point where in all ways it is found in the same condition which the naturally great voice has without study; the study having brought this added advantage, that the student, through the careful tuning of each tone (which brings a voice to balance), has unfolded mentally to the degree that whatever he chooses to do with his voice he can do, and at the same time never disturb this vocal poise. However, in great natural voices the cases are rare indeed in which years of singing and daily use of the voice have allowed it to *remain* in this *perfect condition* in which it is first found.

To explain: When a great natural voice is approached in this manner the vocal condition, so to speak, is laid aside until the mental concept of the pupil has unfolded to the point of directing the use of his tones in such a way that no vocal difficulties will ever arise. (We are still dealing with the thought of production alone). The difference may also be explained in this way—we may give a perfectly tuned grand piano to one who understands music and has musicianship and a perfect finger technic developed, and he will immediately play upon it with artistic results. We may give this same instrument to one who is lacking in musicianship and technic, and he in no way is ready to express what the instrument holds in store for him. Many people with beautiful natural voices are mentally and musically not ready to use them to advantage; and yet these same students may be awakened mentally and musically, laying aside their perfect vocal condition until such a time as it is ready to be used, and then we may say they are ready to play upon their instrument.

Best of all, it is a joy to know that almost everyone who has within him the instinctive desire to sing and who may not have, to begin with, even an octave of musical tones, may have the assurance that when the time has elapsed which is required to liberate and blend the two sets of overtones and bring them to a tuned condition, they too may sing with tonal beauty, which at the beginning seemed utterly impossible.

In this way a vocal adjustment must be developed along parallel lines from the beginning: on one side physically (preparing and tuning the instrument); on the other side mentally (awakening musicianship and imagination); until we reach that point when both lines are complete and blended, and they thus bring to the student this result—the tuned instrument and the artist who will play upon it.

XII

RESONANCE

When a student has reached the point where each tone included in the compass of his voice has been perfectly tuned through this process, he has come to the place where his thought toward his singing, as far as the production is concerned, is exactly parallel to that of the well-developed pianist or violinist. The resources of his instrument are absolutely at the command of his thought. A singer who has been developed through the old way is left entirely at the mercy of all so-called technical difficulties of the music which he is singing, as well as of his own vocal conditions. There is no doubt but in the minds of many of my readers this statement will be instantly contradicted, for we have been educated to believe that when a singer has studied a certain number of years he has, through conscious mental direction and years of conscientious practice and repetition, gained a complete mastery over all difficulties; but, as in the problem of breath control (which is one of the greatest to be overcome in the old approach), not one professional singer in hundreds will claim that he has attained a perfection of breath control.

When we reach the finest analysis of what breath

control in singing really means, we must admit that we find a natural speech condition, reinforced by a full resonant tone. A full resonant tone can only come when the breath control is so perfect (only the amount of breath being used which will start a single speech syllable), that we find a minimum of breath with the maximum of resonance. In other words, in no possible way can breath and resonance be combined. They are *entirely opposed to each other,* and in the proportion that one is present, the other is absent. Singers will always admit that the tone which has the most resonance requires the least breath in its production, and in the tone in which the resonance is most lacking, breath is always in evidence.

Pure resonance is always nothing more nor less than perfectly reflected sound waves. *In no way* does *breath* assist in that reflection. The only possible chance for breath to be used at all in producing the resonant tone is the infinitesimal amount used in *naturally* expressing a *speech* syllable, which is so small an amount it cannot be measured.

The so-called great voices are those in which nature has blended the upper and lower overtones so perfectly that each tone attains its full reflection in resonance; but this condition of balance rarely is used in its perfection because hundreds of years of working with voices *less* than perfectly balanced, have brought with them the custom of *consciously directed breath* and all its attendant ills. Consequently, singers with naturally balanced voices have *never been taught* to use their voices with the marvelous resources which lie within the perfectly balanced and fully reflected tone, *without breath consciousness;* but on the contrary, have been kept in the realm of the usage which has become the *custom,* on account of voices *less* than naturally balanced. Because of voices of this type, the struggle between breath and tone has been considered a necessity in the development of *all* voices. As a result, we hear in all great voices beautiful singing *in spite* of all the limitations that consciousness of breath may bring them.

When we are thinking of the voice as a stringed instrument, we can readily see and admit that all of the most perfect work done by great voices is done on *resonance alone.* The imperfections are always those which can be traced to the consciousness of breath in its application to the perfect natural balance of the voice. In high sopranos of this type, the least consciousness of breath is in evidence because of the great carrying power which we naturally find in the upper pitches. The speaking voice of a *woman* is in the same compass. The bass voice naturally comes next in freedom from all effects of breath, because this lies in the *man's* natural speech condition. The contraltos and tenors are the ones who *suffer most* from application of breath to resonance and natural balance. In the case of contraltos, the voice timbre is farther away from the carrying power of the high pitches and in another compass than the speaking voice. In the tenor voice, the *masculine* speech tones are in another compass from *their* range of singing tones.

Breath consciousness in *any* and *all* voices constantly undermines the natural balance, because it separates the blending of the two qualities or sets of overtones. In this analysis we can prove that *all the carrying power* that any voice needs to perfect it, is found in the realm of *upper* overtones. In the *lower* overtones, we find the unlimited resources of color, depth and emotional content. When these two conditions are perfectly blended in every pitch of the compass of any voice, *all need of breath* and its control is *laid aside. The unlimited resources of pure resonance takes its place,* and fulfills every need of the singer's art.

This point will easily convince the most prejudiced that a perfection of tonal beauty, which is always the result of a fusing of the two qualities, can be attained only when the student is *depending upon resonance alone* for his tonal production; and this resonance needs only the instantly released speech impulse (which naturally starts each syllable) to adjust it to the perfect singing tone.

XIII

BREATH CONTROL

It has been said, there are to be found almost as many methods and ways of proceeding in the development of vocal tone as there are those who are teaching singing, and teachers are able to produce good results in some particulars in almost every voice; and occasionally there appears to be a pupil, regardless of method, who turns out to be an artistic singer.

There are only two points which seem to have been quite generally accepted in methods of vocal instruction—the basic need of breath which is unlimited, and its control. It seems there is the necessity of building a condition of conscious control of the breath throughout the whole compass of the voice. It is to be desired that the great amount of work and time expended in the development of the diaphragm and associated breathing muscles will eventually lead to a condition which is termed automatic, or involuntary breath control, since a perfection of breath control is supposed to allow a singer to use his tones in such a way that no breath is ever in evidence. When all his tones have a maximum of resonance with a minimum of breath, it would appear that eventually a singer might use his voice with a definite understanding of poise and control, which is the goal set before the student at all times.

The insurmountable obstacle which stands in the way of a definite effect in this manner of working, can be traced back to a condition which cannot be separated from cause.

In the universal use of speech activity there is no evidence of breath consciousness, because the breath that is used in natural, spontaneous speaking is based on the *law of vacuum*, and requires no conscious direction associated with its intake and outgo. If we remove the cork from an empty bottle, the law of vacuum instantly fills the bottle with air. It is exactly so with the lung cells.

We all know that when a person is drowned, it is usually said that his death is caused by the water filling the lung cells; or it is *just* as true that it is because the water *takes the place* of residual air in the lung cells. At all times the *residual air* with which our lungs are for the most part filled, is scarcely ever disturbed in our every-day activities; and it is this residual air, which the water throws out of the lungs, which makes death by drowning possible.

The residual air in the lungs is constantly kept supplied with sufficient oxygen through the slight intake and outgo, which is after all the *natural* breathing upon which we *constantly* depend. The muscular movement necessary to adjust this small amount of breath brings with it no sensation. It would seem, then, to anyone who looks into the matter deeply enough to recognize these primal causes and their results, that instead of progress being made by long years of muscular development (which is supposed to be the basis of correct breath control), we are after all traveling in a circle. After years spent in the study of physical development, strain, and wasted energy when the breath control reaches the point of perfection, we find ourselves again at the point where the use of the breath is supposed to be unconscious, and the tone entirely a result of reflected sound-waves, which is resonance. The point upon which all those interested in the training of the voice may agree, is that only in proportion as vocal tones express *pure resonance,* are they wholly satisfactory from the standpoint of musical value.

In the last twenty-five years, the thought has grown much more prevalent that if the development of the singing voice were approached from the mental side instead of the physical, results might be gained with much greater facility. Seemingly, in all cases where vocal development is being approached from the mental side, entire dependence has been put on the *outer ear,* i.e., the student is taught constantly and consciously to *listen* to the tone he is producing, and in all ways to use his intelligence as well as his ears so to direct his production that his tone might more and more approach the ideal which is held in mind. Working along these lines, the teacher is constantly trying to impress upon the intelligence as well as upon the ear of the student, the understanding which will prove to him that he is steadily approaching this ideal.

There is no question as to the value of developing *ideals* in the consciousness of any one who is studying any subject in a constructive way. There is no question but that the holding of ideals and the unfoldment of the finer sensibilities and the imagination, will bring the student power which comes through constructive thinking and intuitive impressions. The difficulty in achieving this mental state while *consciously directing the listening ear* has been proven to be insurmountable, for the consciousness of listening is so closely associated with a reaction in muscular adjustment, which precedes the singing of every *pitch* and of *every change of syllable sound,* that it constantly acts as a *direct damper* to resonance capacity; and the student who is so listening for the results in his tone is thus trying to hold in his thought at the same time *cause and effect,* and thus is working at cross purposes with himself.

If a fundamental cause for the production of every tone is established through the understanding of *release from physical sensation,* to each tone in the making is added the necessary amount of resonance. The student is thus able to lay aside his consciousness of listening, and to *direct all his thoughts* toward the establishment of an entire release of both physical and mental the instant each tone begins. In time, this understanding liberates him from *all responsibility of production,* and because the tone thus liberated is constantly unfolding into a state of perfect tuning, the student need have no fear of effects; for after all, when the *understanding of cause* is great enough in any line of procedure, and the *cause itself is basic,* effects may be safely left to themselves.

XIV

RELAXATION

Over a period of many years, there has been a growing recognition of the influence of direct and indirect interference in every line of human endeavor as a result of nervous tension in some one of its varied forms. This has brought to light the necessity of a counteracting influence which is known under the general head of "relaxation".

In whatever manner the vocal student has been trained, the necessity for relaxation has been agreed upon by the majority of teachers, and he has been told of the need of relaxing the throat muscles, jaw, tongue, etc., etc., which proves that nervous tension in any part of the vocal apparatus has been regarded as being a limitation. However, in this recognition of the *necessity* for relaxation, it seems that the understanding of the correlation of the nerve centers in their sympathetic reactions, one upon the other, is not generally known. If it were, we would not have the fact brought to our notice time after time that students are admonished to relax the tongue while the vocal cords are being kept firm, or to relax the throat while at the same time the diaphragmatic muscles are held tense, or to relax the jaw while keeping up the chest muscles, etc.; for in no case is it possible to liberate *any one group* of muscles from tension through relaxation, and at the same time speak of consciously directing any other group of muscles to remain tense or firm, because *all* nerve centers are so connected in their activity that sympathetic reactions are constantly taking place, which makes such procedure an utter impossibility.

Another point of analysis which seems necessary (when using the opposing terms of "tension" and "relaxation" in their association with the voice and its understanding), is that of the exact meaning of the term "relaxation". When any muscle is entirely relaxed it is found to be wholly inert. Inertia is a deadened state which cannot in any way respond to definite activity. The moment any relaxed muscle responds to activity, it cannot at the same time remain relaxed, consequently the only *possible* value in using *relaxation* at *any* time in *any* part of the body for *any* reason, is for a *period of rest* and refreshment *between* periods of tension.

When we consider, then, that the student is being taught the control of his body and tone preparatory to extreme activity which must take place when the voice and body are used professionally, there remains no possible opportunity to *lay aside* nervous tension *during* that activity. Relaxation, then, is found to be available only during periods which lie *between* moments of activity and tension.

Since nervous tension has been proven to be so great a detriment in all mental and physical endeavor, it would seem that a *new version of its annulment* would be heartily welcomed. This new version of activity brings to us a realization which is many years in advance of the thought of relaxation and *entirely annuls nervous tension* in all forms, at the same time *proving the necessity* of all physical activity being *removed* from the dominion of *conscious mental direction* and its reaction in *sensation.* This can only be accomplished when the body during all its activity is so *adjusted* and *released* from conscious mental direction and sensation, that the spinal column and its muscular structure surrounding the vertebrae is *entirely relieved of all support of the body.*

As long as any muscular support is associated with the spinal column and its nerve centers, we find it impossible to disassociate physical activity of any part of the body from nerve tension in a greater or lesser degree. Up to this time we have not realized that the human body could be *perfectly developed and splendidly poised apart from this spinal support,* consequently the only way out of the dilemma thus far has been by way of relaxation, which in its final state is inertia. Thus we have traveled in circles, *never* arriving at the place where the most extreme muscular activity could be used without conscious mental direction, resulting in sensation and tension.

The important discovery upon which is based the theory of the *Barbereux System,* gives an understanding of the mental and physical reactions and their analysis through which is adjusted the muscular structure on the corners of the back, at either side of the spine, from shoulder blade to hip in a pillar of support, thus releasing the Solar Plexus, sciatic nerves and spinal column from further necessity of consciousness and sensation, which has always resulted from its support of the entire body and its activity. When this posture and poise is established through correct understanding of *Released Activity,* no matter how intense the emotion to be expressed, *nervous tension is annulled,* because the use of conscious mental direction is *never again* found to be a *necessity* in *any* form of expression. *Spontaneity* takes its place.

When any artist in his public work is called upon to depict all phases of human emotion, he is constantly using more or less of what is called "dramatic intensity". The expression of emotional feeling associated with dramatic intensity requires an unlimited use of nervous energy, which in its turn reacts directly upon the nerve centers, resulting in nervous tension and fatigue. Since dramatic intensity must be used constantly by all artists in their expression, a definite, practical understanding of an adjustment which would liberate the whole nervous system from the reactions in sensation, seems the *most important need* of the day. This new vision of released activity *proves we have attained a position of untold value,* when the student or artist can be given a clear understanding of the process through which all normal mental and physical activity may be separated from the nervous reactions of tension and fatigue, which are always the results of physical sensation.

XV

IMPULSES

In order that any piece of mechanism may be made efficient to the highest degree, the problem of *waste motion* is considered a most important one to solve, for waste motion results in loss of power. We may find a parallel to this problem in the activity of the speech organs. In order to accomplish the greatest efficiency in speech activity, each movement of the speech organs must be reduced to its minimum, and in proportion as that minimum results in the absolutely instantaneous release of the sound desired, we have achieved our purpose. This clear understanding of definite, purposeful delicacy of movement without any reaction in physical sensation, brings a *flowing spontaneity* which we seldom hear in the work of speakers or singers, but which is well worth all the hours of mental study and activity release required to attain it.

In order that this type of activity may be applied to any and all languages with equal success, we must seek fundamentals which underlie all languages alike, and in so doing we arrive at the conclusion that in all languages there are syllables, and each syllable has a beginning and an ending. Taking this fact as a basis, we find that to begin a syllable the sound must be released. To end a syllable, the sound must be ended. But we also find that in our thought *the syllable has always been a unit,* the beginning and ending so closely associated as to seem simultaneous. We must now make the analysis of each syllable to prove to us that the first sound must be an instantaneous release which in *no way* uses *formation.* This release we call the first impulse of a syllable. The second impulse (through the use of formation), completes the entire sound of a syllable. Since we have always considered a syllable a unit, instantaneously given, we may be sure that the formation required to give the clear syllable sound in the second impulse, will come with no consciousness of direction—intuitively.

To prove that the first impulse has been released with the correct thought, we must always find the tongue and jaw in the released position as explained in the analysis of the alphabet, the jaw being slightly dropped with a release of the joint, and the tip of the tongue lying lightly on the lower lip on top of the lower teeth. This position, which comes for *a second* with the *release* of the first impulse of *each syllable,* is necessary in order that each set of sound-waves (so liberated) may travel to the elemental sounding board without interruption. This unconscious position of the tongue and jaw liberates all the anatomy of the throat and head, so that they then become conductors for each set of sound waves as they are released from the vocal cords and travel to the elemental sounding board. (All tissues of the body become conductors of sound waves and resonance when released from sensation).

Our conscious thought, then, in its connection with the syllable, needs to be used *only* in the release of the *initial* sound of the vowel which does *not require* formation. Thus each impulse must be released always with a *definite* thought of *detachment.* We call this the "instantaneous release of the first impulse" of each syllable, and as we unfold the thought and the speech activity along this line, they become more and more *instantaneous* in this release. This release at the beginning of each syllable, in *any language,* is an important point which again *proves* the voice to be a stringed instrument; for with this manner of approach we see that each vocal sound is produced true to the form of the principles of a stringed instrument, through the instantaneous release of a new set of sound waves for each syllable uttered, which is thus set free as in the plucking of a string. Many singers in their desire to make a clear-cut attack of a tone have used what is called the "glottis-stroke". In the glottis-stroke, tone results from a conscious muscular clutch of certain throat muscles, the use of which can only bring disaster.

When we turn again to our consideration of the speech impulse which releases a new set of sound waves at the beginning of every syllable, we find a clean-cut, decisive instantaneous beginning for every vocal sound, which brings no physical sensation to any part of the anatomy of the throat, or speech organs. It is merely a natural, spontaneous speech activity adjusted to the finest point of co-ordination with the vocal tone and can only result in clean-cut syllables and tonal purity, which become more and more perfect in their adjustment each time the voice is used.

In using the consciously directed thought *only,* for the release of the first impulse of each syllable and allowing the syllable sound which follows to come naturally and unconsciously, we establish a condition of thought toward any language that might almost be said to give the feeling that one has found a *"new"* language—"a language of first impulses," and as this thought of a new language grows within the consciousness of a student, it is interesting to observe how great a sense of liberty he is given, not only in his singing, but in his every day speech as well. The thought is relieved of so much responsibility, that it has much greater activity and capacity for more essential things.

After all, the formation and production of speech sounds is only a means to an end. The entire importance of the ideas to be expressed in the sentence, is often lost sight of in the labored production of words and tones and the student's responsibility to them, which is the result of the study of diction with the *old* thought. This vision of a new language of impulses gives the student the feeling that he has attained a "shorthand" approach (so to speak), in the usage of all languages, and he then becomes able to conceive the *value of ideas* and their expression, in *proportion* as he *loses the physical sensation* and *responsibility* to *word sounds* and their *production,* for after all, we all need to get a clearer vision which will prove to us that any and *all languages* are only valuable in proportion as they become the *medium* through which ideas may be clearly *expressed.*

XVI

INFLECTION

To explain why it is possible (when one uses the voice as a stringed instrument) for the singer constantly to get the impression that he is speaking with his *natural inflection* in sentences, we must go back to the manner in which *this* type of tone is made. When we speak of the release of the spoken impulse, which starts each syllable, we must remember that first of all the student himself has been taken through a logical course of unfoldment which has prepared him mentally, physically and vocally, to get just *these* results. For so many generations the study of singing has been approached with only the idea of *hoping to get back* to cause.

In this new way of working, each step of progress depends on the student's *recognition* of *"cause"* at *all* times and under *all* conditions. I use this term "cause" in reference to the basic idea of the work which is *vocalized speech.* It will *never* be necessary for him to consider *effects* as such; for in the beginning of his study each of its three phases has been clearly mapped out, and these are wholly dependent upon certain basic laws which are considered as "cause". Consequently, each step of his unfoldment has been a logical state of progress within as well as outside himself, and he not only *knows* the *reasons* for each step, but he *intuitively* feels that what he is doing as he progresses, is the natural result of logical *unfoldment* from its *fundamental* cause. When each of these three phases—unity of thought, tone and action, has fully matured as a part of the ultimate result, the three have become entirely fused and coordinated, which conclusively proves the value of what has previously taken place.

In summing up, then, the use of the spoken impulse of each syllable, the student realizes that from this impulse comes the speech sound which finishes the syllable through the action of the speech organs, and also the tonal condition which is the natural traveling of each set of sound-waves so released, to the elemental sounding board whence it is reflected into vocal tone which instantly expands as pure resonance into space. This separation, so to speak, of the tonal from the speech condition results in an almost unbelievable sense of freedom to the one who sings, for in no way at any time is he reminded of his responsibility toward the production of tone itself, while he is singing—his thought remaining only in the realm of speech, while from each syllable sound that he releases is reflected the resonance which becomes audible to him at the same time it does to his audience, allowing him to realize that each sentence thus spontaneously spoken with natural inflection, instantly expands into beautiful tones which *fill the space* about him, *entirely apart from his responsibility*.

In extreme contrast to this picture, is the one

which portrays the old way of producing speech and tone supported by breath and its constantly increasing responsibility. All vocal sounds based on the support of breath assisted by conscious mental direction, are entirely dependent upon the throat, head and mouth *cavities* for their reflection of sound-waves which result in resonance. This being the case, speech and tone are always conflicting and obstructing the action, one of the other, within the mouth, throat and head cavities. The speech organs themselves can never gain a sense of freedom and independence in their activity, because of the *tonal sensation* which is *constantly and consciously associated with their movement;* and because of this closely associated sensation of speech with tone, we rarely find one who is able to sing with a combination of tonal beauty and diction which is above reproach. So often the tonal condition is sacrificed to gain clear speech, or pure enunciation is sacrificed for the beauty of tone itself.

When a vocal tone is entirely liberated through the complete reflection of the sound-wave (which belongs to it), we find plasticity of movement and nuance in the sound, which is the *perfection* of *inflection* throughout all pitches. Only through a condition which *gives* this freedom may the true individuality of the singer be expressed, either in speaking or in singing.

In the old way of singing, each group of sounds which is contained within the phrase has depended entirely upon the so-called "support of the breath".

This feeling of conscious continuance of tone which a singer must have in order to reach the end of his phrase, has in all ways limited his delivery. In proportion as a voice may have the natural balance, this so-called support of the breath throughout the phrase is less limiting. In listening to professional singers of all types, we but rarely find a singer whose dramatic delivery from the beginning to the end of his phrase proves that he is using pure resonance, instead of conscious muscular control.

In this new way of producing vocal tone, the singer throughout his unfoldment is brought into a clearer and clearer realization that he is constantly using a truly constructive condition, which may be called accumulative. The first syllable of his phrase, bringing its own quota of reflection, *establishes a condition* to which each syllable following adds *its* quota, and the manner in which each syllable reflects the sound-waves which belong to it, allows a greater reflection in the one following. In this way, at the end of the phrase, the singer is given the feeling of a superabundance of resonance, which has come to him in the accumulation from syllable to syllable, until no matter how great the climax he chooses to make, he not only has an unlimited abundance of tonal value and beauty which he may use, but with it has come an unlimited amount of abandon and spontaneity in thought and feeling, which is never found when the voice is supported by breath. With greater understanding, this accumulative feeling is eventually carried from phrase to phrase in the same way in which, elementally, it is carried from syllable to syllable.

Thus a singer, through the daily usage of his tone, and the manner in which he produces it, instead of eventually recognizing the wear on his voice, finds it is constantly building and at the same time adding to his feeling of security and abandon, because of the *unlimited accumulation* of resonance capacity. The voice is thus proved to belong to the family of stringed instruments, improving with age, unlimited in compass, power and beauty, throughout the continuance of normal poise and balance.

XVII

SPEECH MODULATION

The act of speaking well is much more dependent upon the vocal compass than is generally realized, for the tonal beauty of the voice is, and should be, as much in evidence in conversational activity as in the act of singing. To be truly beautiful, a voice should be perfectly tuned. Whether a reader or speaker ever intends to sing or not, is of no consequence if he is brought to realize that no speech condition can be said to be entirely adequate for speech without a background of at least two octaves of perfectly tuned musical tones which will expand into space on pure resonance.

The tonal value of beautiful speech is entirely a matter of modulation, which allows vocal expression to use a wide gamut of tones with such abandon that the result might almost be said to be little *speech tunes.* Every phrase of every sentence expresses true melody through the interweaving of pitch and color, shading and nuance, bringing to our mind bits of beautiful tapestry we have seen.

Quite apart from the ideas being expressed, there is a lasting joy in the work of a reader or speaker who can thus satisfy our inborn love of melody through the flowing tones of his voice. The finer thoughts and sensibilities of an individual are always expressed through these speech tunes, which in themselves are little melodies belonging to the sentence, and yet in entire harmony with the whole group of sentences, one flowing from the other in logical sequence as to tune, melody, and inflection which will satisfy the most fastidious ear.

A reader or speaker thus equipped can realize that diction, pronunciation and enunciation are far more dependent upon resonance for their finest expression, than most of us would believe. When the freedom of the speech organs is understood to be the result of the ability to use them *independently,* one of the other, we can readily see that they naturally and freely adapt themselves in their activity to a tone which is entirely resonant.

Another phase of this independent activity of speech organs is a much greater *delicacy* of movement than when this separation of activity is not understood. So often the appearance of "chewing" his words, or an overabundance of movement of the speech organs in the work of a speaker or reader is most annoying, and is caused by the tongue, jaw and lips *not* being liberated one from the other. When the jaw, tongue and lips act independently of each other, we learn there are only *seven* sounds in the English alphabet that require *any* movement whatever of the *jaw* (all other language sounds depend upon the activity of the tongue and lips). We have never been taught the analysis of syllable and letter sounds in a manner which proves the value of this independent activity. This analysis proves why singers *open* their mouths widely, in producing tone. It is only that they are trying to escape the resistance which comes through the tongue and jaw working together, instead of independently.

XVIII

SPEECH ANALYSIS

In all forms of analysis and study, (in the adaptation of speech to vocal tone), which have been known and used until this time, the activity of the speech organs has not been analyzed nor understood to the point of giving them *independent* activity, which is spontaneous, instantaneous, and without physical sensation.

Wherever any form of muscular activity is used in any part of the body, as well as in the speech organs, *until* such activity is *released from sensation,* it is used with more or less tension and wasted energy; and whenever tension is used in any form of muscular activity, this activity cannot escape a condition of mechanized doing, which once and for all separates the results of this condition from spontaneous, inspirational expression.

The analysis of the English alphabet, which is given in the *Barbereux System of Unified Diction,* in its association with the activity of the speech organs, divides it into five groups as follows:

1) There are seven letters which depend upon the activity of both lips, used at the same time. They are b, m, o, p, y, w, and u.

2) There are seven letters, depending upon

the activity of the jaw, which bring the teeth together. They are c, g, h, j, s, x, z.

3) There are five letters which require only the activity of the tip of the tongue. They are l, n, t, d, and r.

4) There are five letters which depend upon the activity of the back of the tongue. They are a, e, i, k, and q.

5) There are two letters which require the activity of the lower lip only. They are f, and v.

There is a basic condition upon which this release of the activity of the speech organs entirely depends, without which it is impossible to gain the *independent activity* of the tongue, lips and jaw. On each side of the lower jaw there is a set of muscles which fasten the lower jaw to the upper jaw. These are called the "chewing" muscles, which are constantly used in chewing our food. During the chewing process, these muscles are in a state of tension which is necessary to apply the mechanized force which this act requires. This mechanization of the activity of the lower jaw to chew our food, has been carried into all of the jaw activity in speech and singing; and this is the main reason that in producing vocal tone singers constantly use the wide opening and closing of the jaw, which really makes it impossible for the *facial muscles* to respond to the *expression of thought* in a natural, spontaneous manner. At least one half the charm of beautiful singing should be given through facial expression. In the art of acting, everyone realizes this to be true, and this is one of the reasons why the operatic singer does not, and cannot, reach his audience and hold them in the manner that we expect an actor to do. In *Unified Diction,* we are shown the way by which the singer can use his facial expression to the same advantage as does the actor.

The basic condition upon which *Unified Diction* depends is that of the *release of the chewing muscles.* To establish this condition, (which must be kept throughout all activity of the speech organs), we drop the lower jaw slightly open, leaving the teeth apart about half an inch. This position leaves the chewing muscles ready to be active, without tension or sensation; at the same time the tongue lies quietly in an inclined position, the tip lying on top of the lower teeth and touching the lower lip, the back touching the upper back teeth. Whatever activity is necessary for the tongue to use in any letter or syllable sound in any language, can be instantly adjusted from this basic position, to which it returns as instantly when finished. These spontaneous movements are found to result in a minimum of activity, with a maximum of result, and without any physical sensation.

A point of interest just here, is the extreme necessity and value of the awakening, and usage, of the nerve center *under* the tip of the tongue. On the under side of the tongue in the center is what is called the spinal muscle, extending the full length of the tongue. At the end of this muscle (under the tip of the tongue), we find the most important nerve center in its relationship to speech activity, the knowledge and usage of which has been scarcely touched upon. In this basic position of the speech organs required in *Unified Diction,* we find the proximity of this important nerve center and the lower lip established. This means that because of this proximity there is a constant development and sensitizing of this nerve center going on, which is unlimited in its value to all forms of speech activity.

The group of letters which depend upon the movement of the jaw in bringing the teeth together, are the only sounds in any language which require any movement of the jaw. This movement is the gentle bringing together of the teeth from the basic position (which leaves the teeth half an inch apart), and dropping back again in this position. When this basic condition is understood and used, there is no sound in any language which opens the jaw more than this position.

In the group of five letters which require the movement of the back of the tongue, it is really the center of the tongue that is used in this activity, the back remaining in its position against the upper back teeth.

In the group of five letters which require the activity of the tip of the tongue, for the first two, l and n, the tip of the tongue is lifted from the basic position against the lower lip, and touches just behind the upper front teeth. T and d, which follow, start the sound by touching behind the upper front teeth and then returning to the position against the lower lip. In making the fifth sound of this group, r, the movement of the tongue is only the lifting of the tip, curling it away from the lip, and does not in any way disturb the inclined position of the rest of the tongue.

The seven letters which require the simultaneous movement of both lips in the opening and closing position—these movements should be greatly exaggerated, in order to awaken and sensitize the facial muscles which surround the lips.

For the remaining two letters of the alphablet, f and v, which require only the activity of the lower lip, the lip moves from the basic position to the point of instantly touching the upper teeth. These movements should also be exaggerated until the activity is instantaneous and independent.

Up to this time, when one desired to study a foreign language in order to speak it fluently and correctly, one had to master a system of diction which belonged to that language. The fundamental reason for this can be made clear when it is understood that, in the usage of any and all languages, there has been no vision which could prove that every movement of the speech organs used for any sound in the language can be made without muscular tension and sensation. The *Barbereux System* proves without a question that with the understanding of *Released Activity* applied to the speech organs, we find no occasion in any sound in any language to use tension and sensation. This is the explanation of *Unified Diction,* which is adapted to all needs of all languages.

XIX

THE INNER EAR

The "inner ear" is a state of hearing which is closely related to the finer sensibilities and the imagination. Its true value is never realized until its activity is *detached* from the hearing of the "outer ear" through the practical application of released thinking. As is the case in much that is negative in every nature, the understanding of the possibilities of the inner ear yet remains mainly in the realm of conjecture. However, in the development of vocal tone when one is using the principles of the stringed instrument, one is able to *separate* its activity from that of the outer ear, and in so doing it is found to be an invaluable aid in establishing the tuned condition of the whole vocal compass. When this is understood, the singer can direct in the minutest detail all the problems of pitch, melody, interval, power, tempo and rhythm, while in no way connecting the activity of tone production with conscious muscular adjustment and its attendant reactions in sensation.

The *visual* picture of notes upon the staff is partially responsible for the consciousness of high and low in the production of vocal tone, and to this visual picture is also due the early loss of the natural carrying power (upper overtones) in the child voice. To this also can be traced the entire responsibility for all physical sensation and muscular adjustment in voice production, and its deadening limitation of quality, volume and compass. The *outer ear* has always been so closely associated with this sensation of muscular adjustment of the vocal organs, that when a singer realizes he can be liberated from all these limitations by learning to follow the direction of the *inner ear* instead, he experiences at once the feeling of having found a magic key, and the vision of singing with all the freedom and abandon of natural speech thus becomes to him a reality.

XX

THE OUTER EAR

One phase of value to be found in *separating* the activity of the outer ear from that of the inner ear (as far as their relationship to the voice is concerned), is in the fact of liberating the singer from certain effects which the composer has used for the sake of impressing contrasts upon those who listen to the rendition. For instance, we will suppose a passage is written between the B flat below middle C and the B flat two octaves above. In order that the audience may get the impression desired, the passage has possibly been carried out through the use of chromatics, and the group has been made with rests between in such a way that the element of suspension has been carried out from half step to half step until, by the time the voice has reached the high B flat the psychological effect on the audience is that the climax seems at least an octave higher than it actually is written. In myriads of ways these contrasts are presented to the audience throughout a composition, and produce the psychological effect desired.

When a singer's understanding is such, that his vocal production *does not reflect sensation* through the necessity of conscious muscular adjustment, he is able so to protect his own thinking that he *does not* through the *outer* ear get the effect in the same way as does his audience; and he is also able to produce the tones he desires, without the limitation which would be imposed upon him were he listening to his own voice in the same way the audience listens. Consequently, the vocal condition remains as free, and his tones as liberated, as though he were doing the simplest passage within the compass of a few tones.

Composers are at liberty to produce effects, arrive at climaxes, and intensify all these impressions of contrasts through the distribution of pitches, as we have just illustrated, and also through the effects produced by the use of dynamics, rhythm and tempo.

When a singer's vocal condition has reached the stage of adjustment we call "tonal balance" (blending of the upper and lower overtones), his vocal production in no way imposes the slightest responsibility upon him, because each syllable uttered with the thought of speech has brought its quota of resonance, and allows him at all times to approach his singing with no consciously directed thought *whatever* applied to tone or pitch. This, of course, permits his entire attention to be taken up with the expression of the ideas contained in the text and music. This type of expression is called interpretation. No singer is able truly to interpret the text of a song or aria, with the division of attention and thought which comes when he is constantly feeling the responsibility of the tone and its production.

In the old way of singing, we have grown so accustomed to all these limitations, that a young singer is scarcely ever expected to be so mentally and vocally developed that he is capable of giving *his own* interpretation to the composition he is rendering; but usually has had to undergo a long period of study with a specialist in that line who is called a "coach", whose reputation has become established through his ability to engraft *his own ideas* of the *meaning* that the composition conveys, upon the young singer who is preparing for public appearance. Consequently, a young singer *may emerge* from this mechanized type of training with sufficient initiative and originality to express what *he* believes to be the meaning of his text, and in so doing may gradually become a truly artistic singer.

XXI

THE PHYSICAL SENSES

An interesting phase of vocal adjustment, which is found when the voice is treated as a stringed instrument, is that of the *inter*dependence of three of the five physical senses, in their relationship to the production of vocal tone—that of sight, hearing and feeling (physical sensation). We find that as the eye is in the habit of recognizing pitches from their position on the staff, this visual picture of high and low immediately relates itself through nervous activity and reactions to conscious muscular adjustment of the vocal organs. The same reactions take place when the *outer ear* listens for pitch. This conscious muscular adjustment, which is associated with the action of the vocal organs, is our greatest limitation in tonal release and unfoldment. To bring one to the full realization of this fact, we must be willing to recognize the difference between the hearing of the outer ear, and the inner ear. This again brings us to a fundamental *cause* which is entirely mental. Each individual is given the ability to direct his thought consciously, and when thought is used with conscious direction, it is sometimes called the "conscious mind".

There is another mode of thinking which is the

opposite of this: it is commonly called the "subconscious mind". For our purpose we prefer to consider the mental side of this work only, with the following classification—thinking which is consciously directed, or thinking which comes as a result of intuitive impressions.

An advanced movement in education which is at present attaining recognition in all parts of the world proves that within every normal human being, in *early childhood,* are found unlimited potentialities, the nature and possibilities of which in all previous forms of education have been, seemingly, but slightly understood. Throughout all time, education has been based upon consciously directed mental activity, and only in very recent years have intuitive impressions been recognized as a potent factor in education. This advanced vision of education makes clear the fact that the creative impulse in each individual *must be liberated and unfolded,* in order that he may attain true individuality. To liberate the creative impulse in a constructive manner, we must simultaneously awaken and unfold the finer sensibilities. This can be done only through the activity of the intuitive impressions, and through laying aside our dependence upon consciously directed thought and will power.

When we approach the question of the outer and inner ear, *it* may be explained through this analysis. The outer ear is the hearing that is the result of conscious listening, and reacts through physical sensation. The inner ear is the finest sense of hearing, is closely associated with the imagination, and is also one of our greatest aids in the unfoldment of all the finer sensibilities. The hearing of the outer ear, then, may be said to be the result of conscious listening, and thus it cannot be separated from the reaction of muscular adjustment which, in this case, affects the vocal organs. When in the production of vocal tone, the vocal organs are released from sensation, (as they are when vocal tone depends entirely upon the adequate reflection of sound waves), there is no physical sensation of pitch, or necessity of muscular adjustment, from one end to the other of the vocal compass. Thus it is proven, that only the slightest muscular adjustment is necessary between the extremest pitches, so slight an adjustment that the singer himself has no physical sensation resulting from it.

As long as vocal tone is produced through the consciousness of breath and its control, a singer is unable to use this delicacy of adjustment for pitch, which is the natural adjustment. Breath consciousness will always bring a certain reflex of tension against the Solar Plexus, which is the large nerve center near the pit of the stomach (the center of sensation), and in close proximity to the diaphragmatic muscles. When this nerve center of the body is thus affected through any form of muscular reaction in tension, there cannot fail to be a sympathetic reaction in all other nerve centers. The nerve center at the upper end of the spine, being in close proximity to the vocal organs themselves, will transmit this consciousness to the vocal organs as long as the Solar Plexus is affected through the tension of the diaphragm. This is the main reason why no singer is able to liberate his vocal organs *entirely* from sensation during activity, as long as he feels his tonal production is dependent upon breath and its conscious and muscular control.

XXII

OVERTONES

Musicians who in their work are associated with stringed instruments, have an opportunity to gain a very clear vision of overtones and their value. In the family of stringed instruments, it is only through the addition of overtones that depth and beauty of quality and color may come into the fundamental tone; and only in proportion to the perfection of the tuning in any stringed instrument is the quality and color (the result of the overtones) added to that of the fundamental.

When the voice is understood as a stringed instrument, upon the addition of overtones alone do we depend for depth and beauty of quality; and the wider the compass which is included in the tuned condition of the voice, the more overtones are we able to gain in the building of the depth and beauty which is to be desired.

In this manner of voice building, the two sets of overtones, which are recognized as being fundamental, must come into each pitch of the voice, in relation to its position in the scale. It is only when these two qualities are in every pitch, and are perfectly blended, that we obtain what is called a full reflection, which is the entire quota of resonance belonging to the pitch. When this full reflection, (that is, all the resonance of which that pitch is capable), comes instantaneously, the condition then is ready to add the overtones which are the reflection of the fundamental and all its partials combined.

This secondary condition of resonance, called overtones, brings depth and beauty of quality and color which seems unlimited, and as the voice unfolds into maturity through this tuned condition in daily use, there is a constant gain of greater beauty, proving that as long as a normal physical and mental condition prevails in an individual, the voice will continue to improve through constant usage.

This understanding once and for all entirely refutes the idea of the old school of singing, which concedes that very few voices are able to retain their beauty longer than toward middle age.

XXIII

OBSTRUCTION

One word which expresses the main problem that stands in the way of a perfection of vocal balance, or the tuned condition, in any voice is "obstruction". Every normal voice has within it the possibilities of an unlimited amount of upper and lower overtones. This means that in almost every adult voice the lower overtones only are being used. The upper overtones, which are almost if not entirely latent in the voice of every adult, can be completely awakened and restored to activity, with right understanding. The entire release and blending of these two sets of overtones brings the voice to its perfection, because in proportion as these two sets of overtones are blended in every tone of the voice, do we get a full quota of resonance, which is the result of fully reflected sound-waves in a perfectly tuned condition.

To go back to our first point—that of obstruction—we wish to make clear that there are various difficulties which stand in the way of this blending of the overtones, and of their reflection. The main point of obstruction is the outer ear, or consciously directed hearing of tone, pitch, rhythm, melody, interval and word sounds. Each one of these points has been so deeply imbedded in the consciousness of the student as being an obstacle, (because of his untuned vocal condition), that the more he has *consciously* tried to overcome them, the more *serious* has become the obstruction, and the greater his sense of responsibility and feeling of limitation; because all the time the muscular activity and adjustment and the *physical* condition used in the production of vocal sound, has been more and more consciously mechanized and associated with the feeling of responsibility and limitation.

When we go back to the vocal condition of the young child, we can see that underlying all the sounds produced by him is a sense of spontaneity and freedom, which is rarely associated with sound produced by any adult voice. One of the standards of satisfactory tone production, held worthy by those who are interested in beautiful singing, is the ability to produce consecutive sounds with unvarying smoothness. The musical term which expresses this is "legato". When we speak of legato in its association with the sounds of a stringed instrument, we can plainly see that a beautiful legato can only be expressed where there is a superabundance of resonance (the result of sound waves fully reflected). This superabundance of resonance is gained by the unlimited use of the whole sounding board of the instrument. To explain: if we are considering a single phrase of sounds, the first sound of the phrase is so produced that the resonance which is reflected from it does *not cease* to flow, when the second sound is produced; the resonance of the second sound does not cease to flow when the third sound is produced; but because of the perfect tuning of the instrument, the overlapping resonance from one liberated tone to the next immediately blends with each succeeding sound, until throughout the phrase we have the sense of a continuity of flowing sound through all pitches from the beginning to the end of the phrase—a perfect legato.

In the work of great vocal artists we often hear this type of singing, which really comes because of the superabundance of resonance found in the great natural voice. This vocal condition is almost always attributed by singing teachers of the old school, to the use of conscious muscular control of breath and tone.

When production of vocal tone is disassociated from breath sensation, this condition admits of a perfect legato, and is found to be a result of perfect tuning, exactly as it is found in the stringed instrument. It requires no sensation or conscious control of breath or tone, but is a direct result of the unlimited freedom and spontaneity which always comes when the two sets of overtones are perfectly blended and fully reflected—and, as a result, *all obstruction has been removed.*

XXIV

INTERFERENCE

The majority of singing teachers at the present time realize that a vocal tone which is produced without so-called interference, is the correct vocal tone. They also strive to liberate the throat and speech conditions in production.

Good diction is in all cases desired, and the tone which has the most resonance with the least breath in evidence, is considered the best. When a singer's production is easy, and the taking of breath is least in evidence, his work is most enjoyed.

We could go on in this way indefinitely enumerating results which are taken as evidence of good singing—results which the majority of singers and teachers agree upon without question; and yet, when it comes to gathering evidence in different studios in all parts of the world, there are rarely two teachers found who will agree as to the manner in which these results may be gained.

The difference of opinion may, in most cases, be traced to the questions of cause and effect, for the principles of vocal study, as such, are rarely expressed in a truly logical manner as to cause and effect. Most vocal teaching takes effect and attempts to work back to cause. If *cause* were carefully analyzed and decided upon, and *made the basis of vocal study,* it would not be difficult so to establish principles whereby the pedagogy of vocal development could be much more simple than that of any musical instrument.

First of all, two phases of vocal development which have been considered as being constructive when used at the same time, are found to be not an aid but a hindrance one to the other—breath and resonance. Consequently, in seeking a basis for building, (a primal cause), we must first agree as to the type of motive power to be used for the projection and expansion of vocal tone. Is this tone to be that of a wind, or of a stringed, instrument? Let us look, for example, at the instruments used in our orchestra. There has never been used in any stringed instrument a pressure of air to cause the vibration of a string. Since the vibration of the vocal cords represents much more nearly the vibration of the string of the stringed instrument, it would seem reasonable to follow the mechanism of the stringed instrument in its entirety, thus allowing the syllables in our speech to be released in such a manner that, for each syllable uttered, a set of sound waves would be liberated; and in so doing, we would be able to lay aside the host of difficulties which arise when the question of breath, its development and control, has to be taken into consideration. When the consciousness of breathing is taken away from the vocal student, there ceases to confront him, from that time, any and all phases of physical sensation or tonal interference.

The question of breath and its development in vocal study, if consistently followed from cause to effect, brings the necessity of physical sensation from beginning to end. The greatest tonal purity is conceded to be present in a tone where the breath control is so perfect, that no breath is in evidence. Why, then, build up this tremendous amount of physical sensation, muscular control and adjustment in the act of breathing, when the most we really are seeking is tone, which is entirely the result of resonance? This also brings the question as to how *power* may be applied. It may be agreed that pianissimo and mezza voce might depend on resonance alone, but how shall we gain fortissimo, without pressure and control? To answer this question, let us consider the wind and the stringed instruments again.

Is it not the tone of the violin which easily carries above the combined instruments of the whole orchestra? Does not the pianissimo tone of the stringed instrument, perfectly made, fill the largest auditorium with its pianissimo and mezza voce work? Why change the whole character of tone and its production when fortissimo is required? Only because physical control and adjustment in breathing have become so extreme that the whole body of the singer is hampered by it, and can not respond to its reflection and expansion sufficiently (as does the stringed instrument) to bring the fortissimo on tonal expansion, which could easily be made through the reflection from the whole sounding board, aided by the imagination.

We are still seeking cause. The *great* natural voice is the exceptional voice, a few perhaps in each generation. The myriads of voices less than the great natural voice are lacking in resonance, and in proportion as any vocal tone is lacking in resonance, we may feel the need of breath. Consequently, the two have always been combined in tonal production, for it is those voices lacking in balance and tuning which fill the studios of the world. Because a vocal tone must have motive power, unless the natural condition is so great that a perfect balance throughout is the result, we have grown into the belief that breath and resonance must be combined in the building of vocal tone, and that satisfactory results can be gained by so doing.

Along with this combination of breath and resonance, has come the limiting and destructive use of physical sensation and adjustment in all its phases. Voices using this combination of breath and resonance, only succeed where the natural supply of resonance has been great enough to bring the desired tone in *spite of* (not because of) the application of conscious muscular breathing, with its inevitable interference and sensation.

XXV

SENSATION

In the endeavor to lay aside physical effect, and depend upon resonance, many teachers of singing have gone to the extreme of depending upon various physical sensations, which may be associated with the use of resonance in producing vocal tone. For a long time the thought of the student was constantly directed toward the recognition of sensation in the frontal cavities or the mask. This procedure gradually proved to be so limiting to the addition of resonance, and was so often found to produce nasal contraction and reactions in tension of throat muscles, that it is gradually being laid aside. Many times the sensation of resonance *within* the mouth and throat cavities is sought for. This sensation impresses the student with the feeling that he is producing a very large tone, when in reality *this type* of tone is *never* able to amplify in outer space satisfactorily.

Again, chest resonance has been sought for, especially in contralto and bass voices. When conscious thought is directed toward physical sensation in tonal production, from *any* angle, it is most misleading to the student himself, for he is more or less impressed with the fact of his great physical responsibility toward the production, and if he is a conscientious student the greater the responsibility he assumes, the more sensation he feels; the result being finally, that the tone he is able to make is almost if not entirely *enclosed* in the mouth and throat cavities, thus robbing him of all resonance which his voice might naturally possess, and which is required to fill large spaces.

Another disastrous effect of dependence on the physical sensation of tone and its production, is the tension that always results throughout the speech organs. It is next to impossible to express word sounds clearly when the thought of the student is in any way directed toward sensation in tone production.

The emission of clear speech, in singing, is the result of the *independent activity* of the speech organs, and when sensation is being sought for within the cavities of mouth, head or chest, for the *tone,* it is next to impossible at the same time so to libberate the speech organs in speech activity, that pure pronunciation, enunciation and diction are the result. *Exact coordination* between speech and tonal sounds must be *proved* before perfect singing, which is *Vocalized Speech,* can reach its fulfillment.

XXVI

INTUITION

We may be able to approach a great truth from various angles. One of the attributes of a teacher should be the ability to present the same idea in myriads of ways, especially if one is endeavoring to awaken the intuitive consciousness. *Repetition* often seems to allow the intellect to gain a firm hold upon a fact or an idea; but the repeating of the same phrase or the same mental picture, time after time, will only deaden the finer sensibilities, and never allows the unfoldment of the intuitive feeling. Vital, spontaneous interest is an open door to the intuitive feeling, and can only be *kept vital* through a constant *change* of word pictures, which will keep it entirely apart from conscious direction.

One analysis of tonal balance (or the completed condition of the voice, tuned as a stringed instrument) may be presented in this way: When the tone on any pitch is in perfect tune, (the upper and lower overtones perfectly blended to the point of producing a given pitch), it will immediately, on release, bring what we call a full reflection, viz., the entire quota of resonance belonging to it is found within this reflection. In other words, it is perfect within itself, and at the same time is a part of the tuned vocal condition, in the same way that one drop of water is a part of the ocean, and presents within its completeness all that the ocean embodies, in lesser proportion. We also hear as a result of this state of tuning, a perfectly even pulse, or throb, throughout the whole duration of each sound, this pulse or measurement proving the number of sound waves to the second, belonging to that pitch.

When each tone included in the compass of a voice is thus adjusted, we have what we call "vocal balance," and no amount of usage will in any way disturb this fundamental condition of balance, if it is used according to the principles upon which the voice has been builded and liberated. The whole voice is found to be definitely and dependably adjusted to such a degree that the tonal condition is perfectly plastic, and in a so-called fluid state, allowing all that may come to the voice with greater and greater maturity, to be unconsciously adjusted and blended; at the same time the singer has the feeling that he may play upon it with as *sure* results as the pianist knows he will find in the perfectly tuned keyboard under his finger tips.

Having the vocal condition adjusted thus, proves to the singer that for no reason, at any time, will the necessity arise which will cause him to use conscious mental direction for the production of any tone; and thus is liberated his entire mental capacity for use in expressing the ideas presented in his song or aria, and the fluid, plastic state of the tonal condition will thus mirror the varied colors which the thoughts themselves suggest, as the trees on the banks are reflected in the flowing stream.

It has been said by those in touch with the most advanced ideas along educational lines at the present time, that the sum of all education, is the understanding of the best way to bring consciously directed thought in each individual to the point of being spontaneous. This manner of unfolding the vocal condition to its completeness, conclusively proves in the consciousness of every student who arrives at the point of vocal balance, that this state of balance and its effects are not only shown in the expression of his vocal tone, but in any and every line of activity which the needs of his life may express.

XXVII

THE MUSICAL EAR

When a student considers the study of music, one of the first requisites seems to be that of a musical ear. One proof of this condition is that the person is able to reproduce melodies or harmonies he has heard without the knowledge of notes, which really denotes a great gift. This type of talent signifies much more than the majority of people realize, and in unnumbered cases, through the ignorance of the average music teacher in manner of approach, it is more often lost than developed.

One of the points of significance, is a highly sensitized condition of the inner ear. Most people do not know that the ear we use ordinarily in our every-day life may be what is called the "conscious hearing"—or "*outer* ear". This type of hearing is consciously directed, and without it we are very seriously handicapped in the needs of practical every-day life. However, when we look into the matter, and find records of some of the greatest musicians who have been entirely deaf, we are awakened to the fact that there must be another phase of hearing which is certainly quite separate from this outer ear, and is called the "inner hearing".

The so-called inner ear is closely associated with

the imagination and the finer sensibilities, and as yet has not been analyzed to a point of general understanding. It has, however, been proven that there are over three thousand nerves in the inner ear, any and all of which are capable of development in their response to varied sounds; but in the ordinary person during a lifetime there are possibly not more than one thousand of these, and many times less, brought into activity.

The usage of the outer ear is largely through consciously directed thought, and since three of the five physical senses are most closely correlated in their action and reaction, we find they are greatly dependent upon physical sensation, when we make the analysis from the vocal standpoint; thus, in singing or speaking, when muscular adjustments take place which react through sensation, the outer ear becomes entirely dependent upon the physical feeling of that adjustment in sensing the pitch or tone so made, and so is not at all to be depended upon when entire accuracy is necessary.

When we are able to separate the interest of the consciously directed thought and outer ear from the production, it is only through this separation that the inner ear can be associated with the imagination, intuitive feeling and creative impulse; thus eventually it becomes the hearing we use in all creative work, whether it be the interpretation of the work of some Great Master, or some original idea we have held in thought to the point of expression.

XXVIII

SIGHT SINGING

To be able to read notes from the printed page of music is most essential to every student, and though many students of singing are found to evade the issue, and depend upon some instrument to translate the notes to their ear, they will deeply regret in later years that they have done so, for such a weak link in the chain of musicianship will constantly be a detriment to their ultimate success. When a singer can look over a song or aria without the aid of an instrument, and see and feel the significance of every tone, interval and phrase, he has chosen the only way by which sound musicianship may become part and parcel of his individuality.

It is an accepted fact throughout the world today, that every child should become a student of some one of the many musical instruments, as a part of his well rounded education. There is no argument to this statement. However, when the deep significance of the expression of vocal tone and its unfoldment within the consciousness of every child becomes a matter of course, and is accepted as fundamental in his education, his use of an expression through any musical instrument can never take its place, and the unfoldment of the individual will also be understood; for there is no human medium of expression, the source of which is found to be so deeply imbedded in individual consciousness, and which is so closely associated with the intuition and all human emotions, sensibilities and the imagination, as the human voice.

In early childhood, before any consciousness of self enters his experience, he can spontaneously and with entire abandon express all his feelings and emotions via the extreme high pitches where his voice, when understood (through this theory), naturally shows the greatest freedom of emission. When the musical profession awakens to the fundamental significance of this fact, and recognizes it in all its education significance, children in kindergarten will be allowed to sing their little songs in the octave from high "C" to the "C" above, and on through the grades gradually allow vocal expression to take in a few tones lower than high "C", always retaining the freedom of the extreme upper octave as well. By the time children go from the sixth to the seventh grade, they will not have used any pitches lower than "F" above middle "C". This would establish naturally the usage and blending of the upper overtones throughout the whole voice, so that no physical sensation of adjustment for pitch would ever be in evidence.

With this establishment of the natural motive power of the upper overtones throughout the compass of the whole voice, ninety children out of every hundred, when they had passed through adolescence, would be found to have at least two octaves of resonant musical tones, in perfect tune, which they could use as spontaneously as a bird sings.

Another great advantage of establishing vocal tone which is dependent upon resonance alone, during the first twelve years of the child's life, is the elimination of the problem of defective speech as well. The majority of faulty speech conditions, in children of all ages, is found to be almost entirely due to loss of resonance and the independent activity of the speech organs. At an early age the adaptation of this natural resonance of the child voice to sight singing, would prove that all children would learn to read music at sight with splendid efficiency, because of the freedom of their voices in having retained their upper overtones. At the adult age when the study of voice is approached, there would be found no need of muscular adjustment for pitch, which has always been a strong argument of vocal teachers against the study of sight singing before maturity.

All vocal teachers are doing their utmost to establish the free emission of tone, but in most cases, in order that the study of sight singing may not become detrimental to this vocal production, the student must go through a process of establishing such a condition of resonance throughout his compass, that conscious muscular adjustment will not be used from pitch to pitch, which is the result of associating the eye and voice in singing notes from the staff. As long as vocal tones are used which depend in the slightest degree on the idea of breath and its control, the singer is a helpless victim and servant of three of the five physical senses, in his vocal production. The eye picture on the staff constantly tells him he must go up and down; the listening "outer ear" does the same. These reactions from eye and ear come back to the throat muscles, and he cannot escape sensation from muscular movement in the singing of every pitch, while using this conscious muscular adjustment for every pitch. Singers of the old school, who sing well, do so not *because* of their training, but in *spite of* it, with only the perfection of their natural vocal balance used against all odds, and because of this they seem able to surmount most difficulties.

XXIX

MEMORIZING AND INTERPRETATION

In the old manner of memorizing songs and arias, the work was done mostly from the basis of repetition—singing it over and over again—the swing of the melody and accent of rhythm being associated all together with the words and the accompaniment, until an automatic state of thinking made it possible to go through it, without looking at the words or music.

The next step usually included the interpretation, etc., under the direction of a coach. As a result of this type of approach, only very rarely did any student gain the real vision. The *real vision* of expressing the true value of what is contained in a song or aria can *be gained only* through an entirely different approach. In this manner of awakening the understanding to the *basic value* in singing, we approach the subject from quite the opposite standpoint—that of vocalized speech.

To make a simple analysis of the main points which are considered important in the understanding of the adaptation of speech to vocal tone, and its spontaneous expression, we find word and syllable sounds, pitch, melody, rhythm and power (dynamics): five important units which, when understood, supply unlimited resonance to the student of singing.

When a student considers the unlimited resources of words and syllables, he gets a vision of their possibilities in all languages. When he considers the resources of pitch, he finds the contrasts between the extremes of high and low adjusted through the usage of all intervals. When he considers the resources of melody, they unfold the continuity of beauty in contrasts of pitch, rhythm and inflection in all musical forms; the resources of rhythm cover every form of emphasis needed in any composition. The resources of power lie within the gamut between pianissimo and fortissimo, including all uses of crescendo, diminuendo, etc.

The complete understanding of these resources, quickly proves to anyone that any form of mechanized expression would completely annul all their possibilities. This is only another proof that all forms of education, and particularly those of the arts, should liberate and use the activity of the creative impulse and all the finer sensibilities in every line of their work, in order that it may become associated with inspiration.

When a student gains this vision, he will clearly understand that, in the deepest sense, memorizing and interpretation, both of words and music, must go hand in hand. In other words, memorizing words and music through interpretation will give the student the mental pictures, which every sentence and every phrase convey so vividly that he cannot forget them; and this manner of doing, which is the result of the mental visualization that is required to reproduce such pictures, will at the same time enable him to present them as spontaneously to his audience.

XXX

INDIVIDUALITY

We have always taken it for granted in hearing singers, that no mixed concert program should ever be arranged with two of the same type of voices—two sopranos, or two contraltos, or two basses, or two tenors. In fact, it has been considered very bad taste to place any two of the same type of voice on the same program. In making an analysis of this opinion which the public has toward singers, it is quite interesting to go a little deeper than the surface to find a *reason* for this attitude.

In proportion as an individual is able to express himself with true spontaneity, he expresses his true individuality, which is often confused with the term "personality"—many times the terms being used synonymously. A clear definition of the two is often expressed in this way: Personality may be what one *appears to be,* individuality is the expression of what one *really is.*

When we are thinking, then, of the expression of individuality, the most potent factor in that expression is through the voice, elementally of course, the speaking voice. In proportion as the voice that has been used in speech has been entirely liberated, do we get the expression of individuality through the speech sound. Few adults, however, are able to use their speaking voices with this abandon; but in spite of the restrictions that we hear in the expression of most adult voices, we are yet able to feel the individuality more through the speaking voice than in any other way. It is true that so often we will hear it said, "I do this or that naturally", when in reality it is only that we do this or that *habitually*. In the activities of most adults we find very little that comes spontaneously, on the impulse, but nearly everything habitually, through having used that manner of doing so long that it seems natural because it does not require conscious direction.

This brings us to another point of interest—the difference between natural, spontaneous activity and automatic activity, which is the type used by most of us all the time. Whenever we *consciously* repeat an act a sufficient number of times, it becomes automatic, and requires no further conscious direction. This sort of action is never spontaneous and can in no way express individuality. Whatever we do or think which has come through conscious repetition may seem natural, because the necessity for conscious direction has been laid aside.

When we go back to the expression of individuality through the vocal tone, (which should be our most potent means of expression), we find that the voices which have undergone the longest years of so-called training are those which express individuality in the least degree, because this training has been along the lines of repetition and conscious direction, which can only result in mechanization. In this manner, each type of voice becomes fixed in its compass and production, and our feeling is that to hear more than one soprano voice, or two at the utmost, on the *same* program would be very monotonous. This is true. We find it in all these different types of voices, and this fact proves most conclusively our theory that when, in the unfoldment of the voice, we are working entirely with the thought of liberation, *true individuality* will *eventually* be expressed, and we will find as great a variety in comparing the work of two sopranos, or two contraltos, as between voices of different types; for no *two* people have the same characteristics, the same features, the same manner of speaking, and consequently vocal training should *liberate* and *accent* these individual differences and traits, until no two voices of the same kind would express monotony in consecutive hearing.

XXXI

FACIAL EXPRESSION

In observing singers of all types, it is quite surprising how few are found whose facial expression is natural and sincere throughout the tone production of the entire voice. To express ideas through speech before an audience, we realize there is only the occasional person, the expression of whose face intensifies and radiates the thoughts his speech conveys. Let us find, if we can, some of the difficulties that lie in the path of those whose work it is to impart thoughts amplified and radiated by the singing tone, and thus we may, step by step, come to a deeper recognition of the greatest difficulties that confront the singer in this particular phase of his work.

We realize through our study of the muscular structure which covers the area of the face, what unlimited possibilities for activity lie throughout this muscular mask, and which in most adults are allowed to remain practically dormant from early childhood as a result of many years of self-consciousness and suppression.

If it were not for the expression which comes through and around the eyes, there would be an entire lack of animation and activity in many faces. Beauty specialists the world over have endeavored to bring plasticity to the muscles of the face through massage of various forms, but there is no denying that the activity of the muscles themselves—when *liberated* to *independent* activity—responds to the thoughts and ideas being expressed in speech, and lend to the whole countenance animation and variety which is most satisfying to look upon. Through the action of the lower jaw, we find the only means of expression in many faces. From the line of the mouth upward over the face there is no means of movement except through the muscles which underlie the skin, and since the upper jaw does not move, there are comparatively few people who use their upper face and lip and all facial muscles above, with any abandon or freedom of movement in speech activity. The main reason for this state of inertia of the facial muscles, as we have previously shown, is that of self-consciousness.

From year to year as we emerge from childhood, most of us learn to suppress and disguise our innermost feelings at all times, and because of this the face itself finally becomes a mask behind which our real selves hide, peering out at the world only through the eyes. Every individual, if brought to the realization of the advantages that will come to him through the awakening and liberating of his facial activity, not only in personal appearance but in the development and radiation of his individuality, will leave no stone unturned which will bring him this realization. By people who are not preparing for a public career of any kind, the value of this understanding might not be appreciated; but no young man or woman can afford to take his or her place in the world, in any line, without constantly striving not only *to be,* but *to appear,* at his or her best. It is so often the case that in our association with people, we are much more influenced than we realize by a countenance which is filled with animation, and upon which we may see the reflection of mental activity clearly expressed.

Those of us who are following the study of singing, find the *observation* of singers in their work as interesting as is the listening, for in facial expression may be found almost as great a power of interpretation as in the tones themselves; and until a singer is able to express, with all sincerity, through his *facial activity,* his true individuality, he has not reached the place where he is able to express the full meaning the composer had in mind. It is rather disappointing, however, when we make a close analysis of the facial activity of professional singers in general, to be compelled to admit that the greater degree of their facial movements does not come from the thought which is being expressed, but from physical limitation in their production of tone. Of course, the action of the speech organs is most prominent in singing, and we have so long accepted the idea that in proportion to the opening of the jaw a tone is beautiful, that we have *ceased to expect* the natural expression of speech about the mouth in singing.

In noticing the mouths of singers, then, with this

thought in mind, we can readily see that there is no human expression found necessary in the portrayal of an idea in a song, which would at any time necessitate such an unnatural opening of the mouth as we see throughout most singing. The singer, however, is in no way to be blamed for this condition, unpleasant as it appears, because he has been taught that his tone proceeds *out* of his mouth, and of course the natural conclusion is, the larger the opening, the larger the tone. Since there are places in each number where large tone is necessary, the mouth falls into the habit of opening widely on the slightest pretext. If any singer would go before a mirror and open his mouth in the same manner that is done in singing, and observe the unnatural effect it makes in its reflex action over the entire face, he would certainly think the matter over seriously before again appearing in public. Even the expression of the eyes becomes strained and unnatural when the mouth is opened to its utmost.

There are few people who can realize that in every day speech there are only seven letters in our alphabet which require *any* movement whatever of the jaw, if the jaw is released from sensation in its activity. We have grown, even in speech, to be so accustomed to this unnecessary activity of the jaw, that without it the facial expression seems lacking. We then begin to realize that when the muscles underlying the whole face are liberated from self-consciousness in their activity, and when the lip action is what it should be, we feel no lack in facial expression if the jaw performs its function of liberated speech activity, and no more.

XXXII

FALSETTO

There has always been a question associated with the tonal condition called "falsetto". Many teachers and singers consider this usage of voice, as being wholly legitimate and permissible especially for piano and pianissimo work with upper pitches, whether the voice be masculine or feminine. On the other hand, it is a type of tone made use of by singers who appear to be limited in certain directions, and because of this there has grown to be a feeling that it is rather a fictitious or untrue type of tone, which singers of reputation hesitate to employ.

The falsetto tone, primarily, is found to be a tone that is robbed of its maturity, a spurious condition only in the fact of its not having become complete. The fundamental condition of falsetto is correct. First of all it is entirely easy to produce. It can never bring destructive results so far as strain or force are concerned. It is a sound that is started legitimately through the reflection of sound-waves, but wherever it is employed, one can be certain that the sound-waves used in its production are given no opportunity for full reflective amplification or radiation. When any vocal sound is started through the activity of sound-waves in such a manner that it is fully and instantly reflected, it becomes a truly musical tone, properly expressed. A sound may be started in this way, but because of limitation of one kind or another, is not fully reflected and cannot adequately fill spaces according to acoustical laws, through expansion, radiation and amplification. When this is the case, a tone thus limited is beyond the power of a singer to enlarge, and is called falsetto. Thus it may appear to be musical and fill certain requirements in a song or aria, but one has the feeling that in some way it is separated from the legitimate tones that are used throughout the rest of the compass.

We often hear falsetto notes in tenor voices, which are considered to be the most difficult to adjust in the upper end of the compass, and it is often possible for a tenor to use certain arias which are higher than he can sing with legitimate tones; so by using a few falsetto notes for the extreme pitches, he is able to render them with the desired effect.

It is to be regretted that the general public has grown to depend upon the *compass* of a voice for its classification. If a woman has high pitches, she is designated a soprano; if a man has low pitches he is classified as a bass; if a woman easily sings low pitches, she is a contralto; if a man's voice has high pitches he is called a tenor. In reality all voices should be classified as to *timbre,* not compass.

When we approach the voice as though it were a stringed instrument, we may readily see that the classification should be through the analysis of timbre alone, and never compass or range. In finding our illustrations in the family of string instruments, no one would ever confuse the tones of a violin, cello, viola and harp, even though the same composition were played upon each one consecutively. We would judge only through the timbre, and so we find it when voices are adjusted through the understanding of pure resonance alone, which is fully reflected sound waves based on acoustical laws.

An added advantage, however, which the human voice has over the characteristics of stringed instruments, is that each individual who sings has his *true individuality* to express through the *timbre* of his voice, and that when this individuality is fully amplified, we at no time would be conscious of monotony if several sopranos sang consecutively, or several contraltos, or basses, or tenors, for in each voice the individuality of the singer would create sufficient variety, aside from the timbre and type.

XXXIII

EMPHASIS

When a composer is adapting music to a poem, he has many aids at his command. His first thought is to bring out the meaning of the words of the poem with natural, flowing emphasis. This emphasis of speech, is the most important point in any and all forms of interpretation, whether it be for the dramatist or the singer. When we listen to expressive speech we realize, with analysis, that emphasis is achieved in many ways. In speech, we have always admitted that inflection is the most important point.

By inflection in speech we refer to the nuance, which simply expressed, means the movement of the voice through different pitches, and also with variations in power and color. It is interesting to observe that in the speech of cultured people, there is much inflection. In proportion as culture is lacking, we find less and less movement of the voice through varying pitches, until those of the most illiterate and uncultured type often used almost a monotone in their speech expression. To be sure there are exceptions, as there must always be, in making sweeping statements which relate to the human family.

To go back to the composer of songs, in his adaptation of speech inflection to the melody he has in mind, he is permitted to use many forms of emphasis—tempo, which gives him longer or shorter duration for the words in a sentence; rhythm, which brings the accent on specified words or syllables; pitch, which opens to him unlimited opportunity in the matter of intervals; modulation (in its free movement from one key to another), which again gives unlimited opportunity for all types of emphasis and expression; and last, but not least, dynamics, which simply expressed means every possible gradation of power from pianissimo to fortissimo. All these he uses, primarily, that the story or narrative expressed in the poem be given dramatic completeness, the worth of which is measured in its relation to art by the truthful simplicity the musical setting allows the words to convey.

When the student of singing approaches the interpretation of a song or aria, there are at least two requisites which he must have at his command, the vocal and the mental. Mentally, his equipment should be adequate to the clear understanding of the ideas to be expressed through his singing. A long, careful study should be made of the poem quite apart from the music. If his education and culture have led him in the paths of good literature, if his observation of human nature in its various reactions to specified conditions has been cultivated, if his finer sensibilities have been awakened and he is filled with love of humanity as well as the love of his art, he will be able gradually to become imbued with the spirit of the song; and this alone allows many singers, in whom the vocal condition is most inadequate, to so hold an audience in conveying the thought of the song to them, that entire satisfaction is the result.

As to the vocal condition—we will not for a moment specify the type of voice the singer is using. We will not consider the method of his production, as such, but will consider him in the light of the performer, who is to play upon his instrument (with the speech activity) so that the mechanism becomes merely a keyboard upon which the thought may be expressed. At the beginning of vocal expression, as applied to singing, the singer as well as the composer finds his most important point to be that of emphasis. Through the work of the composer he finds the adaptation of the words to the music to be such, that he also is given unlimited use of tempo, rhythm, interval, melody and dynamics, so perfectly adapted to the poem in hand that if he is so fortunate as to be able to grasp the full meaning of the words, he may then without self-consciousness, and with natural speech inflection, together with the aid of the flowing tone, which in its unlimited hues of color is reflecting his every thought, be using what every great singer realizes is the ideal condition for singing—*Vocalized Speech.*

In the analysis of recital work being done by the many singers of note today, it is most interesting to endeavor to select those who in the greatest measure carry out this ideal throughout a recital program. Many singers of note, to a surprising degree, depend almost entirely upon the *emotional* uplift of the moment to carry them over the greatest difficulties of their program; but singers who do this, are those who are known to have had unusual natural voices before the study of singing was taken up. Consequently, although great risks are run through depending upon what they feel is emotional intensity, there is always left to them a dependable, fundamental condition, which remains in *spite* of the training which they have undergone, not *because* of it.

XXXIV

UNIFIED DICTION

The study of diction and speech analysis, as usually taught, touches upon pronunciation, enunciation, phonetics, and so forth, and has been approached from varying points of view. Great stress has been laid upon the conscious practice of vowels and consonants, of words and syllables, in all possible combinations; the thought of the student always being directed toward great muscular activity, much repetition and drill. In many cases, this mode of approach resulted in clear enunciation, much precision, and a definite manner of speaking, which seemed to prove results were satisfactory. Students of dramatic art (as a class) usually, in their endeavor to enunciate, impress the hearer with the feeling of a stilted, mechanical mode of speaking, which in years past was taken as being proof that the student was professional and well schooled.

In recent years, our attitude has changed toward speech expression of those in professional work. The pendulum has swung to the other extreme, and we now realize that when the greatest art is expressed we get the feeling of entire *simplicity* and *naturalness,* abandon and spontaneity—that the actor really is the character he is depicting; and while the need of clear speaking and fine enunciation is as great as ever, yet the *manner of doing it* can in no way appear studied or pedantic. This change of attitude brings with it the realization that the study of language sounds, and their expression, must be approached in some *indirect* way so that we may get results without retarding or limiting, in any degree, the *natural conversational flow* of words and phrases on pure resonance.

Few people realize the entire *inter*dependence of the action of jaw, tongue and lips. There are only seven letters in the English alphabet which require *any* movement of the jaw (if the jaw is independent in its activity). These are the letter sounds which bring the teeth together. The majority of people, even speakers and singers, use some jaw action (with sensation in the "chewing" muscles) in almost every speech sound uttered, because they do not realize that each of the speech organs may be *wholly independent in all its activity,* and thus its action need never reflect in any physical sensation whatever, at any time, in any language.

In the study and expression of all languages, the speech organs have never been adapted through independent activity. Because of this, each language has to be approached through a mechanized condition of the speech organs, in order to attain the proper accent, inflection, and clarity in delivery. *Unified Diction* is instantly adaptable to any language and to all the needs of that language (since all activity of the speech organs is spontaneous, instantaneous and without sensation).

When we are awakened to the value of this *independent* activity of the three speech organs, without sensation, we begin to realize how much wasted energy and motion there has always been in the old way of consciously adjusting the speech organs, with their *inter*dependent action. Every movement of the speech organs done with will power drive, results in a shock against the large nerve center at the top of the spine, and is a tremendous waste of so-called nervous energy and motion in any and all languages.

N. B. See detailed analysis in Text Book "Vocalized Speech".

XXXV

ACOUSTICS

Every person who makes of singing a profession, and all those who sing occasionally for church or concert, are more or less affected by the size and shape of the room in which they sing. Even singers of years of professional standing, find it most difficult to adjust their voices to the size and shape of the auditoriums in which they perform from night to night, en tour; and this fact alone becomes to them a real problem, and many times is the only reason that they are compelled to admit they are "out of voice" on some particular occasion. Voices whose training has been such that they are dependent upon conditions *outside* themselves for the full reflection and expansion of their tone, in order to obtain sufficient resonance, are the ones who suffer the most deeply from these conditions. When the size and shape of the room afford them a sounding board which happens to be adjusted to their individual needs, they find they can do their best singing; but unfortunately in the profession, few singers are able to sing in the same room continuously; consequently, they are at the mercy of acoustics, good or bad.

The most efficient way to surmount this difficulty, is that voices be so understood and adjusted *during their study* that for their focus and amplification the body of the singer, when used as a sounding board, is found to be entirely adequate for the reflection and expansion of sound waves. This manner of production allows the singer to feel no responsibility for any tone beyond the instant it is emitted, reflected, and associated with space. Vocal sounds thus used, and dependent upon the syllable impulse alone for their instantaneous release, follow so closely one upon the other, that an overlapping stream of resonance is flowing away from the singer and adequately amplifying into the space which the room affords, be it any proportion, large or small.

This type of emission will give the feeling to the audience that the whole room is completely filled with musical sound which does not seem to come directly from the singer, but creates the impression that the tones are following one upon the other as do the circles in a quiet pool of water, after having been set in motion by the dropping of a pebble.

Another explanation of this type of vocal tone may be given in comparing sound with light. The space which is enclosed in every hall or auditorium may be said to be already filled with the ingredients of both sound and light. The air enclosed in the room is ready to become tone the instant it is associated with the movement of sound-waves. The ether with which the room is also filled, is as ready to become light, when associated with the movement of the light wave. In turning on the electricity all the ether in the room is instantly set in motion by the manner in which the power of electricity sets in motion the light wave.

The singer who knows the way by which each syllable that he utters instantly liberates a set of sound waves, and will as instantly, when reflected, fill surrounding space with musical sound, is the one to whom the problem of acoustics ceases to be a problem; and in the same way and for the same reason, the tone of the stringed instrument is always found adequate in filling an auditorium of any size or proportion, and is always clearly heard above the combined sounds of the entire orchestra.

XXXVI

MIDDLE VOICE

In approaching the vocal condition of the adult for the sake of a greater development in song or speech, many teachers have considered the middle voice the proper field for elemental work, having the fear that to go higher or lower than a seemingly natural compass would cause strain that might eventually bring destructive results. There is much to be said for and against this manner of approach. Those in favor of it feel that the voice with which we sing and the voice with which we speak are one and the same, and that by beginning in the realm of natural speech expression, we are less likely to encounter the fear of pitch and the tension which results therefrom.

If the student in question has what is called a natural balance (a perfect blending of conditions which bring quality and power), this mode of training often times seems to bring satisfactory results; but on the other hand, a student who has this natural balance, will in all probability find his way out into good singing, in spite of any type of training, for this natural balance makes beautiful tone possible over a fairly wide compass; because the resonance which is a result of natural balance is ample, the speech condition is fairly free, and the student has never felt the limitation of pitch consciousness and all its attendant ills; and so in expressing himself upon the subject, he can say with perfect honesty, "I have studied with many teachers, and many different methods, but it seems to me I have worked it out by myself."

If a student's work proves to him that he may use parallel lines, he is able to take advantage of all the good points and lay aside the difficulties of the wrong, in almost any manner of training. When he is working along parallel lines—on one hand the tonal value is gradually being brought to a tuned condition through the release of an ever-increasing capacity for the reflection of sound-waves (the result of which is resonance), and his speech condition is being liberated, which is also adding to tonal freedom.

On the other hand, his mental capacity is being awakened and unfolded through his growing understanding of the value of discrimination between conscious direction and that which is intuitive and creative, and also through his ability to liberate the mental from the physical, in its activity; and thus he is gradually unfolding the state of mental and physical balance which we call poise.

XXXVII

INCENTIVE

There is an attitude taken by friends, and especially by parents, which stands behind the incentive for music study in general, and that of singing, in particular. It is this: The only excuse for such procedure, is the expectation of a public career. To this attitude may be directly traced most of the tragedies which occur from year to year in all the great cities of the world, tragedies which become known only to the participants themselves and their immediate family and friends.

When a student begins the study of singing with a public career in view, unless he has an extraordinary voice and an unusual equipment of character, talent, health and ambition, to him is usually held out the expectation of becoming a church or concert singer. A pitiful aspect of these conditions, when one knows the truth of the situation, is that rarely even in the large cities do churches pay a living wage for a solo artist, and outside of concert work and vaudeville there is small if any opportunity for so-called concert work. Of course, radio and moving pictures are also a limited field, in recent years.

If students would only observe for themselves in these matters, they could easily arrive at the conclusion that only the greatest vocal artists—those who most often have gained fame in operatic roles—are the ones whose reputations warrant concert engagements which are financially adequate; and even many of the singers of this type combine with their singing a certain amount of teaching, in order to make a comfortable living. The thousands and thousands of boys and girls who leave comfortable homes in all parts of the United States, and flock to the cities for the sake of engagements or for the carrying on of years of study in preparing for public work, with a public career as their ultimate goal, is almost beyond belief.

People in general have very little idea of the unwritten, everyday tragedies which are the result of this lack of understanding of a situation where statistics show that rarely more than one, out of every ten thousand who study from five to ten years with conscientious endeavor and legitimate ambition, *ever* attains public recognition. Meanwhile, the nine thousand nine hundred and ninety-nine, because of this professional expectation, in no way fit themselves mentally or physically for the myriad opportunities in all parts of the country, for them to become leaders in their community away from publicity and footlights, and because of this general misunderstanding, they eventually fill the ranks of the musical derelicts. The booking offices in every large city can testify that to them these disappointed ones surge in droves, season after season, from office to office, seeking for enough employment to furnish them a meager existence, because through their experience they have been so warped from normal living, so disappointed in life and its possibilities, so cheated of a natural trust in mankind, that it is impossible for them to adjust themselves to normal living in any community away from the cities, and adequately fill the places where a high standard of manhood and womanhood would bring them success.

This mistaken idea of a professional career before the footlights as the only incentive for music study, is the source of these tragedies and the deadly disappointments which underlie them. Humanity must be awakened to the fact, that a change of human opinion can be gained only through the recognition that the study of music should become *basic* in the *education* of every individual, and as necessary to his *fully rounded development* as the study of mathematics. We will have to grow into this more advanced vision through positive proof being given by all musical educators, that when the study of music in general and of singing in particular, is understood in its true relationship to the unfoldment of all the finer sensibilities in each nature; and when its power to liberate the creative impulse, the intuitive impressions, the imagination, and by so doing readjust thinking from its latent to its full grown possibilities, is known, we then may realize how practical and great an aid it can be in giving each individual a deeper appreciation of all the beauties which lie about him, wholly unseen and unrecognized by most of us, and through which the little joys of the every day may invigorate and support our ideals and allow us to regain and retain our normal poise, above the deadening effect of the commonplace.

XXXVIII

ITALIAN METHOD

This question is often asked of students and teachers: "Do you use the Italian method, or do you believe in the open throat in singing?"

The so-called Italian method, in its purity, embodied the ideas of those old masters whose years of teaching experience had been gained through working with naturally balanced voices, for it is conceded by the musical world, that more voices of that type have been found in Italy than in any other country. The Italian temperament combined with the Italian language, in which the vowel sounds predominate, has seemed to present fewer obstacles to good, natural production; and when we hear an Italian voice of this type pouring forth a wealth of color and quality, with its superabundance of resonance, its seeming freedom from all muscular interference, it is no wonder that their standard of beautiful singing has been kept for so many centuries.

To make an analysis of this condition from our point of view is quite simple—really a natural blending of the two qualities (two sets of overtones) throughout a wide compass, the same quality that has been found in all the great voices of every generation, voices that have been able to adapt themselves to a grand opera repertoire with no vocal adjustment found to be necessary, only the learning of the music, as has been the case with most of our greatest singers.

When a vocal sound is produced through resonance alone, to the one who is singing as well as the one who listens, the impression is that of unlimited space; for whenever vocal sound travels without obstruction, on expansion, from the natural sounding board (or reflector), it results in this feeling of space. The impression we get in hearing voices of this type, is that they are using an open throat. In asking a student to reproduce consciously this condition of space in the head or throat, we are defeating our purpose, for the sensation and impression of space can only come when mental direction and physical sensation in the production of vocal tone have been entirely obliterated.

Tones of pure resonance, which expand in space on their own motive power, give the effect of unlimited space, both to those who produce them and to those who listen, merely because in tones of this type we get no effects of obstruction.

XXXIX

VOCALISES PRO AND CON

In the choice of material used in the study of singing, it has always been considered necessary to use many vocalises for the elementary work, gradually adding songs and ballads in the compass of the middle voice, and finally after several years of study, an occasional aria from opera or oratorio.

When the student following this mode of procedure happened to have a beautiful natural voice, well blended and in tune throughout a compass of two or more octaves, this type of material seemed to be entirely adequate. However, the majority of voices that fill the studios of the world, are those that have much less than two octaves of compass, and usually more or less of an untuned tonal condition throughout. In voices of this type, resonance is generally lacking in all pitches and particularly so in certain parts of the voice. Working along the old lines, voices rarely seem to attain more resonance. In a few the uneven condition is to a degree remedied, while the majority, in their endeavor to gain more power and compass, lose more or less of their natural beauty of quality in so doing. Voices of this type rarely get to the point of being able to do arias creditably, and consequently the goal held out for them is that of being a church or concert singer.

In the *Barbereux System* of releasing voices, as the first step in voice study, we re-establish the condition of the octave of sounds which comprise the child voice. These are the pitches beginning four or five notes higher than any vocal sound the adult student is in the habit of making, and may extend above that point an octave or more. This mode of procedure adds to any voice not less than an octave of sounds above what is considered its natural compass, but in order to establish this condition the student must be given a thorough understanding of the manner in which it is to be done, for if any of these pitches are used, accompanied by any *physical sensation whatever,* detrimental results would follow. Consequently, the student is allowed to do them only with the teacher's guidance, and so entirely in the child manner of production that they are instantaneous, spontaneous, and result in no physical sensation. It will readily be seen that vocalises, as such, cannot be used to any advantage in this mode of procedure. The work at this period might be likened to the tuning of a stringed instrument, each tone individually liberated to its full quota of resonance through adequate pitches, with and without words and syllables, but each tone always separated from every other tone at the time of usage.

Since it is only resonance upon which any musical tone may depend for its full quota of beauty and power, all elementary study is devoted not only to the gaining of individual resonance for any pitch, but to the full understanding of a constantly growing reflective capacity for resonance, which in its turn, as a background for the whole voice, furnishes the quality and color which can only be the result of using all the overtones of which each particular voice is capable. Eventually, a compass of from two to three octaves of evenly tuned musical tones, is the result of this manner of working, and then it is found that the only music which includes this compass in its highest musical form, is that of grand opera and oratorio. Consequently, all voices are given those masterpieces which belong to their particular voice, which are used as a means of unfoldment and tonal expression in the same way that vocalises were used by the students of the old school; with the added advantage, however, of musicianship and repertoire and the greatest familiarity with the best music written for the voice.

As a result, every student gains familiarity with these masterpieces in the same way and for the same reason that a student of literature must have an understanding of the works of Shakespeare, which are the greatest of their kind.

XL

PARALLEL LINES

In the unfoldment of the voice according to the principles of the *Barbereux System,* the work proceeds very clearly along two lines simultaneously: on one hand the tuning of the tonal condition, which consists of eliminating conscious direction and physical sensation,—until every tone in the compass of the voice instantly receives its full reflection in resonance; and on the other hand, the mental release which comes through the knowledge of how to keep the consciously directed thought away from the ever-changing physical conditions, which accompany the tonal adjustment. During this time, throughout every change of condition, the student is able to recognize and classify all the obstructions which he meets, whether they are vocal or mental.

Forms of consciousness most important to be eliminated in our study of singing are those of pitch, rhythm, melody and words. The forms of consciousness we meet in the physical condition are those of jaw, tongue and lips, and many which result from consciously directed breathing. When tones are made which depend on the support of breath, every change of pitch or syllable brings its reaction in the form of some consciously directed muscular movement, which becomes an obstacle to reflection of sound waves. Thus it can readily be seen that when the vocal condition, as such, has reached the point where the student may feel no responsibility whatever for the production, he has gained the poise which enables him to feel the freedom in singing which natural, spontaneous conversation may bring. This means that the muscular adjustment which takes place in producing any word or syllable is so slight, that it results in no physical sensation. Any and all muscular movements of the body may be thus reduced to a minimum when they are removed from conscious mental direction, and given independent activity, apart from tension.

Through the instantaneous release of the first impulse of each syllable, we remove conscious mental direction from the production of sounds in any language. This enables each syllable gradually to gain full reflection in resonance on all pitches. When all pitches are produced with their full reflection of resonance, we have eliminated pitch consciousness. Thus, step by step, along these parallel lines, one constantly aiding the other, until the student has reached the place where his voice appears wholly apart from physical sensation in production, and through the freedom of his language, he is enabled to play upon it in space (as upon an instrument) with his imagination.

There are many conditions to be met in this vision of unfoldment, which in themselves seem quite simple; and yet, because of this simplicity, it is easy to confuse them through the conscious direction of thought. For instance, it is comparatively simple to learn to release the impulse of the syllable. It is also comparatively easy to consider that each phrase, instead of being expressed in a melody upon pitches, may be expressed as a spoken sentence. When the student uses his language of impulses, combined with the thought of the spoken sentence, his results are always satisfactory. If, however, the thought of the impulse is associated with the consciousness of pitch, he will fail to get satisfactory results; or, on the other hand, if he fails to use the impulse and considers the whole syllable instead, with the thought of a sentence, he again fails in his result. It is only the combination of the *impulse* with the *thought of a spoken sentence* which will bring the *full reflection in resonance.*

XLI

BALANCE

Balance is the poise of proportion. To remain equidistant from all points; the sum of all endeavor; a scale by which painting, music, sculpture, architecture, literature, human lives, and human character, may all be measured. We may also apply this mode of measurement to the one who sings. He must express the tuned instrument, the perfect balance of high and low quality (overtones), which means that within each separate tone can be found unlimited breadth, depth, richness, clarity, carrying power. The proof that the singer has attained this vocal balance, is that his work appears to be *Vocalized Speech*. That he expresses sincerity, spontaneity, simplicity and abandon in all phases of his work; that the working of no mechanism is in evidence; that one's attention is not drawn to modes of facial expression, physical positions, or the act of breathing, in any form. Plasticity, which results in refinement and grace of attitude, movement, and expression, must be revealed; also, simplicity of purpose, and authority, which are the results of having so established all conditions pertaining to his tone and diction, that no mannerisms may ever detract from the message being delivered.

We can also say in a larger sense that these results, so much to be desired, are brought within the reach of the singer through the full unfoldment of his spiritual, mental and physical possibilities, for the reason that the physical body must have become balanced throughout all activity (without sensation); that the mental capacity must have attained its completeness; that the spiritual nature should be unfolded; each having attained balance in its own realm, in order that balance may be found between the adjustment of each to the other. When this completeness has been attained, *all consciousness of self* has been *laid aside,* physical and mental, and the singer through his intuitive impressions may come into *close association with inspiration,* without which, after all, no form of art, in the truest sense, can be expressed.

XLII

COMMAND VS. CONTROL

In what is commonly called vocal development, which follows the plan of the old school of teaching, we are constantly confronted with the word, "control"—control of breath, control of power, control of quality, etc. In fact, the thought of conscious control is constantly held before the student throughout all his development, and to him eventually it seems that the sum of all good singing, may be found under *this* head. Familiar words have a significance brought to them by long usage and association, and many times because of this, their finer shades of meaning are entirely lost sight of. Primarily, the word "control" signifies a host of difficulties, which may be handled successfully in proportion to the will power used—difficulties which are entirely destructive if allowed to escape the vigilance of the one who has the case in hand, but which at any and all times are to be watched constantly and handled with force and determination.

When vocal unfoldment is carried out through the principles of the stringed instrument, we find a word which takes the place of the word "control" and signifies an entirely different state of mind toward the voice and its usage—*"Command"*.

Instead of the word control, then, which we find

so much used in its association with the work of the old school of singing, in this type of singing which we call the "new way", and which is entirely dependent upon resonance and its amplification, we make use of the word, *"Command"*. When this word is used in this association, the meaning carries with it the deepest significance.

We take for granted, first of all, that all of the battalions stand marshalled ready for instantaneous activity, only awaiting the direction of the officer in charge. This demonstrates the fact as a foregone conclusion, that every possible preparation in making ready these forces has been completed; and since the work of preparation is completed in every detail, these forces stand individually as well as collectively, not only ready to follow directions, but willing and eager to hear the word of command.

When we consider the various phases of unfoldment which must be followed to their maturity in the work of a singer, we can begin to realize how much it means to the singer himself, and the feeling he has toward his work, to know that not only individually has each line of understanding been followed to the point of completion, but they are all ready collectively, as well, to accept the slightest direction of his thought. Thus, when we speak of a singer, as critics often do, singing "with authority", it means just this—that he not only has control of his forces, but they stand at last wholly prepared and willing to do his bidding. They are at his "Command".

XLIII

CORRELATION OF THE ARTS

The correlation of the principles which underly all phases of art, is an interesting study for anyone engaged in art expression. Sculpture, painting, architecture, music—in proportion as their development and the principles upon which they are builded express truth, all rely upon the same basic laws. In a general sense we know this to be true, but in a specific sense, comparatively few artists in any line go deeply enough into the basic laws of their work to find this correlation between what they are doing and what is being done in other lines of art expression.

In speaking of singing as an art, we realize superficially that this is true, but in the unfoldment of the human voice how few have been able to trace back to fundamental laws, and prove in every respect that the liberation of the vocal tone is entirely according to the laws governing art expression in other lines. First, any work of art, in order to ring true, must be builded according to the laws governing art expression in other lines. Any work of art, in order to ring true, must be builded accordding to the principles of Contrast, Proportion, Unity. An artist has the inherent right to use the greatest possible extreme in expressing his idea, and to use every medium of expression he has at hand to gain contrast, provided, with this unlimited freedom, he does not violate the laws of proportion. This being true, the result can be no less than unity, which is completeness in every detail.

Second, art is supposed to be an expression of Ideals—the vision we may have of perfection. Since the human soul constantly hungers for beauty, it seems that the Ideals of art have striven mostly for the expression of beauty, which is a result of completeness. In architecture, how much of the uncouth and the elemental is visible in a structure until it is finished? In sculpture, first comes the rough, unhewn block of marble, from which the artist gradually expresses the perfection of his ideal, in statue form; the artist in no one particular dwells upon finish until the whole has been completed—last of all completing the details which bring the effect, which we call beauty. In painting, first is the rough sketch of the drawing, the layer after layer of color, until the last touches of shading and blending bring completeness, which is beauty. In all these various lines of art expression, the greatest extremes are sought first, then the proportion which brings the unity that in its completeness of perfection, is beauty.

In the study of the human voice, which we will call the "instrument", we must use as our main medium of expression, sound. Along with this, we have brought to us by the student all of the characteristics which he as an individual embodies—spiritual, mental and physical. All of these characteristics may be called our structural material, as elemental, as far from the perfection of adjustment, and as fundamental, as the piles of steel and concrete which lie outside the structure being builded, or the unhewn block of marble, or the untouched canvas and the paints upon the palette.

Within this unlimited supply of building material, which we find in the individuality of every student, there is rarely found the exact proportion of each which the well rounded artist, in the unity of his art, must express. Before the tonal condition itself can be completed, much must be supplied through the unfoldment of these characteristics which lie latent within him. During the time that the tonal condition itself is under adjustment, if we are true to the principles of art, we dare not touch upon the side of beauty, in any particular, until all the elements which the instrument has need of in its completion, have been supplied through release and adjustment. In other words, tonal beauty (without which in its fullest perfection singing cannot be classed as an art), can only come through the well rounded development of every capacity of the individual, and until every possible avenue of contrast attains proportion, only then, do we get the vision of completion —which is Unity.

When we come to the decision that the human voice may be understood from the basis of its being a stringed instrument, we are shown in all ways that it is a simple matter to correlate our work with art expression in other lines. Through his own release and unfoldment, the teacher must have a vision which allows him to see the possibilities of a beautiful voice in each individual student, in the same way that in the imagination of the architect the completed structure stands; in the imagination of the sculptor the beauty of his statue is waiting to be released from the marble which surrounds it; in the imagination of the painter the picture is finished, only waiting for the medium of paints and canvas to bring it as clearly and completely to our vision as he already sees it, within his own consciousness.

XLIV

STANDARDS

In the expression of all the arts, except singing, there have been established through the years accepted ideals in the doing of certain things which have thus become "standards", so to speak. We go back to them when we need measurement of values in the judgment of an artist's work, and often the ability to measure up to these same standards becomes the price of an artist's success.

Progress means that these accepted standards gradually evolve as we advance, yet in the keeping of the ideals fundamentally pure, we have made it possible for their influence to retain an established value in our cultural life; throughout these readjustments they have kept their hold upon our finer sensibilities, and our appreciation of their ultimate worth has deepened with the passing of the years.

In order, then, that singing may be classified as an art, and have at least a few standards of measurement by which an artist may be fairly judged, by both the critics and his audience, it seems that the profession would be justified in their establishment.

Take for example the vocal tone, apart from the singer and his personality, as one would classify an instrument—does the artist express a compass of perfectly tuned musical tones? Does each tone of his voice show a uniformity of resonance throughout, as does a perfectly tuned stringed instrument? Does he use delicacy of touch, spontaneity and abandon? Does his work express sincerity of purpose? Are his extremes well balanced from fortissimo to pianissimo? Does he use legato and staccato with equal freedom; also diminuendo and crescendo? Does he use a well poised mezza voce? And are pronunciation, enunciation and diction up to a certain standard of measurement? Are facial expression, bodily posture, and grace and dignity of bearing in evidence?

A few standards such as these may be used in the analysis of the work of all singers, quite apart from the charm of individuality, which in the estimation of critics and the public at large weighs so heavily in the scale *for* or *against* the work of every singer.

XLV

THE PRESS

At once the most formidable obstacle or the greatest help to the career of the singer, is the version of the Press held by the public in general and the musician in particular; and in many cases this version of the situation seems to hold good.

If it were possible to have a standard of judgment established pertaining to professional singing, and all artists would abide by these standards, we could then consider that criticism or praise might each be more just. We also must take into consideration that the critics, themselves, are often more or less limited by the policy of the paper for which they are writing, and many times because of financial need they may be susceptible to the persuasion of financial gain. We must also realize they are only human and cannot always lay aside a personal bias of opinion, which is caused by their own natural reactions to a performance.

It seems that the safest course a singer can pursue, in view of these difficulties, is to have so thorough an understanding of his own shortcomings and be so honest with *himself*, that he will stand as his own severest critic, and in the face of all praise if he does not come up to his *own ideals*, will in no way be influenced by it. On the other hand, if the criticism is against him and his analysis of his work *truthfully tells him* he has done *his best,* and he is able to be as impervious to *blame* as to *praise* because of such recognition of values, he is sure of constant growth and advancement; for more careers are undermined through undue praise than by adverse criticism.

When a singer has reached the point in his unfoldment, through which his whole desire is to express clearly the ideas the words convey, and can lay aside all consciousness of self and keep his vision wholly liberated, in so doing—which is a logical result of a thorough preparation in technique and musicianship—his work should be convincing and capable of steady, consistent progress.

XLVI

FINISH

In any work of art, "finish" is understood to be the addition of the last touch given to every detail, and if this last touch adds to the completeness which gives us entire unity, we may be sure such finish is according to the laws which govern art expression.

Finish must also express the completeness of balance, without which true unity is not in evidence. Finish that gives the last touch to the extremes of contrasts, without destroying perfect proportion, can only result in unity, for when any work of art rings true throughout its expression to the laws of Contrast, Proportion and Unity, it stands justified.

In the association of the term "finish" with the work of singers, we often find that its true meaning has been misinterpreted; for, in examples of vocal expression, often that which is understood to be finish is found upon close analysis, to be a layer of artificiality which has been acquired by the singer's use of voice or diction which otherwise would be quite in evidence.

If the laws of art expression were adapted to the use of finish in singing, as in other arts, finish would be found to consist of the logical completion of certain ideals which have been followed consistently throughout the entire period of unfoldment.

When the adjusting of a voice consists in giving each tone throughout the compass its proper tuning, every point to which finish can be *honestly* applied is only an entire completion of every detail. In no way can artificiality or imitation, be found adaptable.

Aside from that of his instrument, the progress of a singer who hopes to become an artist is found to be from *within,* and if during his years of study his thought processes have become so refined, his discrimination so keen, that his sense of values is never disturbed; and if through released, constructive thinking his emotional nature is balanced with his imagination, the result will be a finish which is the most exquisite completion of every detail, as in other lines of art.

Throughout the years in which music in all its branches has been studied, the student of singing has not been given a clear understanding of the analysis of the law of acoustics, and the unlimited resources such analysis can give to vocal tone and its production.

The *Barbereux System* presents a new vision of the art of singing, which is entirely dependent upon the logical unfoldment and practical application of the science of acoutics adapted to every phase of the singer's art, and supplying every need of the human voice, whether used for singing or speaking.

Note: The foregoing Essays, appearing in Manuscript form, copyright 1927 by M. Barbereux-Parry.

PART II

VOCALIZED SPEECH

"THE SINGING OF THE FUTURE"

A TEXT-BOOK OF THE BARBEREUX SYSTEM
FOR
STUDENTS AND TEACHERS

THE HUMAN VOICE—A STRINGED INSTRUMENT

(Discovered by M. Barbereux-Parry in 1900)

When we affirm that with the understanding of the *Barbereux System*, vocal sound for the first time in the history of music, is understood and produced in every detail according to the principles of a stringed instrument, it remains for us to prove it.

Through the science of acoustics (upon which the understanding of all musical instruments depends), we are able to apply practically in every detail to the voice and its production, in this Work.

There are only three essential points to consider in the production of the tone of a stringed instrument. First step, the perfect tuning of the string. In the application of the stringed instrument principle to the production of *vocal tone*, "the first step", (the tuning of the string), vocal tones must be so liberated in the production, over a compass of at least three octaves, that upper and lower overtones will adjust to a state of perfect blending (which we call becoming tuned), *in every pitch*. This must be done without reactions in breath, or tension or physical sensation in any part of the body.

"The second step": a set of sound-waves is liberated from the tuned string by an instantaneous touch. For this instantaneous touch, which liberates a set of sound-waves from the tuned string, the *vocal* application is made through the understanding of the *independent* activity of the *speech* organs (tongue, lips and jaw).

When we use the initial sound of any syllable in any language, via the independent action of the speech organs, and the spontaneous expression of speech sounds, we are able to *liberate* a *vocal* set of sound-waves in such a manner that it is exactly as *free* as the set of sound-waves which leave the harp string with every touch.

"The third step": this liberated set of sound-waves must be instantly reflected from an adequate sounding-board. When a set of vocal sound-waves is *thus* liberated, it instantly travels to the elemental sounding-board, (the inter-osseous spaces—the back of the skull) and is as *instantly reflected* and expands into space on pure resonance

The results gained from this understanding are unlimited power, compass, color and beauty, with perfect inflection, shading and nuance, and with all the spontaneity and charm of artistic speech expression.

In summing up these results, we prove singing to be VOCALIZED SPEECH, The Singing of the Future.

EMPHASIS

By M. Barbereux-Parry

When emphasis is associated with language and vocal sound, it becomes a source of supply for the variety so much needed in all forms of expression.

We are quite familiar with the emphasis which comes through rhythm (fast and slow); we are also familiar with the emphasis which comes through pitch (high and low); we are also familiar with the emphasis which comes through melody (which is the musical form of inflection).

Beyond these basic forms of emphasis lie an almost unexplored region of charm and beauty through the expression of tonal color through inflection, through modulation (which is a form of inflection), and through pause.

When these finer forms of emphasis are understood and associated with the basic forms we speak of, we begin to hear ideas presented with a pictorial vision, which may also be considered as unlimited in its possibilities. The greatest vocal artists have used all these forms of emphasis naturally and intuitively, but without the undertanding of a basic analysis.

This manner of approach, language combined with expression, which we call VOCALIZED SPEECH, presents and makes clear the use of a principle which every student may thoroughly understand and gradually express in a constructive way throughout his whole course of study; which not only adds to the beauty of his tone, but to the unlimited vision which we find in the work of a few of the greatest vocal artists.

CONTENTS

PART II

Vocalized Speech

Vocalized Speech

I

RELEASE OF SOUNDING BOARD-REFLECTOR

Activity Release

In the study of the voice, there are certain principles which we wish to establish in our consciousness, in order that our viewpoint may be in harmony with the principles of this work, and that continually we may keep before us its ultimate end and aim.

We must first of all establish the fact in our minds that the voice is a stringed instrument, and being so is dependent for quality, compass, power, and all its attributes, upon resonance alone. Resonance is the result of reflected sound waves. Resonance, then, is dependent upon a sounding board from which it may be reflected. Broadly speaking, the sounding board of the voice is the whole body. In order that the body may become a sounding board we must first put it into a normal condition. That is, as soon as possible, through the *release of all activity,* we must strive to adjust the body symmetrically in every way —first, that it may express perfect poise, grace of deportment and bearing, and through this condition may be the better reflector for sound-waves.

"Activity Release" from the viewpoint of normal unfoldment alone, is most necessary. Most of a singer's life is spent before the public. Any development which adds to the personal appearance is most essential, and the well-proportioned, perfectly poised body, dignified carriage and graceful activity, means to the singer almost more than we can estimate in his success before the public. It is true that few singers appear in opera, but if one intends to use his voice only in church or recital, it means quite as much as, and sometimes more, than it does to the opera singer, who has in his delineation of character every opportunity to disguise his personal defects.

Corrective Breathing

In order that lung activity in a human body be normal, we must first of all recognize the position of the lungs. The lungs lie on a perpendicular line directly in front of the spine, from underneath the shoulder blades to just above the waist line in the back. There are various sets of muscles which actually control the action of the lungs. In other words, we may learn to expand the lungs in different directions through control of different sets of muscles. This conscious direction of the action of muscles controlling the lungs is always limiting. In their complete or natural action, all natural activity of the lungs is unconscious.

Describing Lungs, etc.

For many years singers and speakers have been taught to believe that through conscious control and development of the diaphragmatic or abdominal muscles, great lung action, control and expansion may be secured. The muscles of the diaphragm are closely associated with the solar plexus (the sensory nerve center of the body). Conscious muscular control and development of the diaphragm results in the sensation of great expansion just above the waist line, coupled with a feeling of conscious power. This sensation, when applied to breathing, has been generally supposed to prove to a singer or speaker that he had inflated his lungs to the fullest capacity, and that through this feeling of conscious power applied to the muscles of the diaphragm, he would be able to control the outflowing of the breath in its relationship to tone and speech. This manner of lung development and control is called diaphragmatic breathing.

There has been another theory which is called abdominal breathing. In this manner of breathing, conscious muscular control and development has been called for from the diaphragm downward across the whole abdomen, and was supposed by reason of the greater area covered to result in even greater power of control over the lung action. If any thinking person who is truly interested in correct breathing, will study human anatomy to the point of analyzing the position of the lungs in their relationship to diaphragmatic and abdominal muscles, he will quickly decide that as far as their direct application to the lungs themselves and their action is concerned, this theory is wholly a fallacy.

All muscles of the torso are more or less affected indirectly as the result of correct lung activity, but consciously localized control of muscles of abdomen or diaphragm as a cause for correct lung expansion and control, may be easily proved to be wholly wrong.

When a deep breath is correctly taken, as in the case of a young babe (which example has often been cited by those advocating diaphragmatic or abdominal control), it is true that the entire body gently expands and contracts during the process of breathing but as in the case of the young babe, this should be an unconscious reflex action throughout the whole muscular area, not a conscious localized action of any one set of muscles.

To reach the seat of lung expansion clearly, and without using localized muscular action, we should first stand erect. Standing erect from the viewpoint from which we are working, means to allow the back of the neck and the whole spine to be on an incline from the head to the hips of about 45 degrees, so that the arms will hang loosely forward from the shoulders. This position also results in a loosening and letting go of all the diaphragmatic and abdominal muscles, and the loosening of the muscles of the hips, knees and ankles controlling the joints. The shoulder blades in this position are quite widely separated. The muscles surrounding the pit of the stomach seem to be almost collapsed or caved in. While the body is thus hanging loosely forward, direct the thought to the area underneath the shoulder blades in the back and take a full breath, which will result in a pulling apart of the shoulder blades. In other words, we feel lateral expansion, which seems to stretch the body at right angles under the arms and around under the shoulder blades. When *in*haling, the shoulder blades slip apart. When *ex*haling, they should return to the natural position of being close together.

Inhale and exhale naturally through the nostrils. Direct the thought across the back and on to a level with the arm pits, first slowly, afterwards rapidly—more like panting, with great freedom and release of muscular action. In breathing in this manner, we should feel no forward movement of the diaphragm in front and no raising of the chest. We go through these movements only to awaken a concept of *natural* lung activity which annuls the old idea.

If we stoop over far enough in this breathing activity, and loosely enough, we will recognize that the muscular action which has resulted in lifting the chest high with the *up* and *down* motion will not be evident, for the *lateral* expansion will take its place.

In using this activity for lateral expansion with the thought directed between the shoulder blades, we will gradually find that the lung expansion from this point extends downward to the waist line in the back, gradually building out a condition of muscular activity along each side of the spine from the hips to the arm pits, which we may call the *back* corners of the body. This condition of released activity results in a new state of poise and endurance for the entire body, because first of all it acts as ample support for the spinal column in that part of the back which is usually considered the weakest, and in that part of the spine throughout which lie most of the great nerve centers of the body.

In other words, when localized diaphragmatic action has been developed, we find this state of muscular development on the *front* corners of the body, extending from the waist line on each side of the stomach, to the arm pits. This we find most abnormal in professional singers, and when this development is evident, with the high chest which usually accompanies it, we will generally observe that there is a hollow between the shoulder blades in the back and a great lack of development from the waist line to the shoulders on each side of the spine, a condition which is commonly called "sway-back". This position is also accompanied by a roundness or seeming enlargement of the shoulder blades, a stooping forward of the neck where it joins on to the body, which results in a double chin and a large protruding stomach and abdomen.

The theory of this System of breathing and physical release, being so utterly at variance with the theory of either diaphragmatic or abdominal breathing, will be very difficult of acceptance by many who have previously believed in the *old* ideas of breath control; but if anyone will carefully follow these directions of released activity for six months, the great changes that will take place in the release and poise of the entire body, and the feeling of freedom throughout the region of chest and stomach, will easily convince the most skeptical.

It is difficult to imagine how the upright figure and fully developed chest may result, but with the using of this activity it will be found that high chest development comes most naturally from the natural unfoldment of the normal lung activity, which is attained through this lateral breathing. In other words, the constructive condition of the building of the high chest *goes on underneath* the structure of the chest, and in this way develops a *permanent* poise of the chest that is high and full, and is not dependent upon the *act* of breathing in any way.

If in no other way it would be possible to convince the prejudiced person of the value of this System of Released Activity as compared to the old schools, the comparison of the fully developed body resultant from *this* System, and the development of the body of almost any professional singer, is quite convincing. The conscious development and control of the muscles of the diaphragm and abdomen rob the human figure of every line accepted by the rules of art as being truly beautiful: the protruding stomach and abdomen, the curving out of the back across the shoulder blades to the hips, the stooping forward of the neck from the shoulder line, and in maturity the line of the lower face wholly lost in the abnormally full throat or double chin, which results from the conscious raising of the chest. All these go to prove that aside from the art of singing or speaking, the truths that we learn from the art of sculpture, at least, are wholly obliterated through abnormal development.

These release movements also *fill* the hollow that lies between the shoulder blades, giving the body that flat back and full chest which is understood to be the ideal concept of the fully developed human figure, at the same time leaving the muscles of shoulders and diaphragm so loose and free that even while one is standing seemingly erect, the shoulders feel as though they were drooping forward a trifle.

Let us analyze the position of the lungs for a moment, and we will see why it is so essential not to allow conscious tension through the diaphragmatic muscles during the act of deep breathing. The lungs are parallel with the spinal column. This brings the base of the lungs within an inch or so of the outside of the body in the back, directly beneath the waist line. It is here that the thought should generally center in the act of deep breathing. This gives the sensation of lateral expansion, which pushes apart the shoulder blades during the filling of the lungs; and while we may *miss* the up and down motion of the *chest* that comes from lung expansion wrongly directed, we will soon see that the building process of muscular development is from underneath, and is slowly but surely adjusting the appearance of the chest so much to be desired by those seeking correct bodily poise.

If, on the other hand, the thought is directed beneath the Solar Plexus, involving the diaphragm and its surrounding muscles, it results in a conscious action which in reality does not aid in the expansion of the lungs themselves, but only results in an abnormal development of all the muscles and tissues of the stomach and abdomen. A form of activity which will aid in all conditions is to let the weight rest on the balls of the feet, letting the shoulders hang loosely, allowing the body to stoop forward from the hips until the arms hang from the shoulders in a perpendicular line. Inhale slowly while the sensation comes of spreading apart the shoulder blades; and exhale, allowing them to come together. If this is done with proper regularity, the arms will swing regularly back and forth as the breath comes in and goes out. All this activity which localizes the act of breathing is used only to annul gradually the *previous* ideas of activity, and to allow normal activity which is *not* localized and does not react in *physical* sensation.

The Solar Plexus

Down through the ages, in all times and in all generations, it has been conceded that with all the inventions of the human family there has never been a piece of mechanism, as perfect in its possibilities and functioning, that in any way can compare with the perfection of the human body. It has been used, misused and abused in every conceivable way, and yet each normal child that comes into the world brings with him intact all the latent possibilities which were given to the earliest generation.

These are a few main facts which are generally understood and accepted when the body is analyzed and classified according to human understanding and beliefs, viz: heart action and circulation and breathing. The nervous organism, with its center of sensation (the Solar Plexus) and the association and coordination of these most important means of activity, through what is called nervous energy.

When we observe the young child (before he has become conscious of himself), we find the perfection of spontaneous activity, so perfectly balanced and coordinated that never for a moment is his thought connected with his body in this activity, for as *long as he remains apart* from self-consciousness, all his activity does not invite his interest or attention in any way, and his body is practically being used without reactions in sensation. It is so perfectly balanced that no nervous reactions are connecting up with the Solar Plexus, (without which there can be no sensation). We marvel at the tireless energy of childhood—this is the answer.

When this is understood in all its deep significance, we will *protect* the realm of childhood from any and all conditions which *awaken* self-consciousness, will power and resistance; thus the child may go through his life with all the joy which spontaneous, sensationless activity will bring. This would be using what has been called the "ounce of prevention" for most of our problems in life.

A message of encouragement and hope may be given to the adult *at any age*. Through this approach to all activity the adult body can be released, reclaimed and readjusted through this vision of spontaneous, sensationless activity, by using ten to fifteen minutes a day in the movements given for release and adjustment.

In all study of the human body in adult activity in so-called physical culture, gymnasium, athletics, etc., we have depended on all activity being used between the "upper and nether millstones" of force and resistance, thereby with every movement wasting at least half of the nervous energy used in the action. We have only considered the extremes of tension and relaxation in all our analysis, for every movement has reacted against the Solar Plexus and thus resulted in physical sensation, which means waste of energy.

We must again allow all the muscles of the body their right of *independent* activity, for at least half of the muscles of the body have only been used through resistance, and of course resistance is tension. When we are using all the activity in a *balanced* manner, there can be perfect coordination and no reactions in physical sensation, for no message is ever taken to the Solar Plexus except via tension. When all activity becomes balanced, it also becomes spontaneous, and we find no drive of will power, no resistance and sensation—the perfect activity of early childhood regained.

Released Activity Movements

Explanatory of the necessity of keeping up the Activity Release from the very beginning of the voice work, there is no direct connection made between the two lines of unfoldment, until throughout the whole vocal compass all pitches are fully reflected.

This unfoldment proceeds in two parallel lines. The voice becomes the tuned scale, and the release activity movements, through being done daily, are gradually releasing all activity from reactions in sensation and tension. In this manner the whole body becomes a conductor and a reflector of sound-waves and resonance. Unless this point is clearly understood by the student, it is very easy during the first two years of voice work to neglect this daily activity. When these two lines of unfoldment are carried out simultaneously, by the time the *voice* is *ready* to reflect sound-waves, the released spinal column becomes the conductor and thus the whole body becomes the reflector.

When the voice is being expressed through the principles of the stringed instrument, this set of release movements must be done once or twice each day. If students are careless and omit the regularity of this preparation, (while the voice itself is becoming fully tuned), we will finally realize that unless the full *capacity* of the *sounding board* has been established, the voice will come to a standstill and the student will have to wait at least a year or two to make this preparation that is necessary. When the voice starts to unfold in this manner (being wholly dependent on sound-waves and their reflection), it is an absolute necessity that we constantly add to the capacity for reflection that is needed to liberate the *added* sound-waves which come as a result of balance and maturity.

N.B. A clear understanding at this point must be given to the student, of the recognition of the *manner* in which these movements for release are to be done. The temptation to go through physical exercises, as we have always done them through conscious repetition of each movement for a certain number of times, *must* be *entirely laid aside* and *disregarded.* In these movements for Released Activity, the second movement must follow the first, and so on through the complete group, without repetition, to gain results. The whole group may be repeated not more than twice a day, once on arising and once on retiring.

In doing these movements for release, we are utterly reversing all that has been believed and done in the old forms of physical exercise. When a movement is taken to release the activity of the muscle, or sets of muscles used, the more *slowly* it can be done, the greater the advantage if the thought is kept objectified, apart from the body, while the movement takes place. A feeling of gentle reaching liberates the muscles during these movements in the manner that eventually will give them their balanced activity, without sensation. When each set of muscles in the body is thus liberated during its activity, it becomes wholly independent of reaction in tension and thus gradually is our body brought to a state of balance and coordination. This spontaneous sensationless activity brings the same joy to maturity that is found in early childhood, before we became conscious of self.

Movements for Activity Release

(These movements must be done slowly and thoughtfully at least once a day)

Preparation of the body: Stand in the center of the room. Release Solar Plexus (pit of stomach). Release sciatic nerves (hip joints). Flex joint of knees and ankles slightly. (The triangle of tension). This bending of the body across the pit of the stomach, and of the hip joints, with the flexed knee and ankle, liberates the weight of the body until it rests on the balls of the feet.

N.B. It is most important that following each set of movements and before starting the next set, this position for releasing the triangle of tension should be taken.

Lift chin upward, as though head swings on a pivot which extends through the neck at the base of the ears. Gently tip the head from front to back on this pivot. In using this movement we realize that the *head sits on top of the neck* and should move freely without any neck movements. (This liberates the nerve center at the base of the brain, at the top of the spine). Using this position of the body, which allows it to fall forward from the hips at an angle of 45 degrees, while the face is gently lifted and the knees and ankles flexed, results in liberation of the three main nerve centers—Solar Plexus, sciatic nerves and nerves at top of spine—from sensation during all activity movements (triangle of tension). Through this position we are liberating the body from the triangle of tension which we find is established in every mature person, the beginning of which can be traced to the activity of the body in so-called deep breathing, that has always been advocated through all forms of physical action.

The First Group Movements consist of six positions:

1. Count slowly, 1, 2, 3, 4. On the first count place feet close together in *parallel* lines; second count, right foot placed a foot away from the left foot (*parallel* position). This allows all muscles on the inside and back of the legs to become liberated from resistance through gentle reaching. Third count, same position as first. Fourth count, same position as second. This reaching position extends from the hip joint to the heel, leaving the right leg in a diagonal position and all weight of the body remaining on the left leg. Retain this position while lifting the left arm from the side (not from front or back) from the shoulder, at full length above the head. Let the back of the hand fall on the head. From this position allow the wrist to take the lead and reach the left arm upward in a diagonal direction. This gives a diagonal reaching position from the right heel to the left wrist across the back, and

brings into gentle activity all the muscles of under arm and under leg and the unused muscles across the back of the body. If the drooping position of the body is retained throughout the reaching process, at the end of ten seconds of reaching in this manner, allow the arm to fall from the shoulder as dead weight and the right foot to come back to first position.

2. Second movement, same as first, using opposite foot and arm.

For the next four movements of this group take position in the center of the room, which allows you to use the four corners of the room as focal points.

3. Count as before, 1, 2, 3, 4. On first count, feet close together. Second count, right foot extended the distance of about a foot toward the right front corner of the room (right front diagonal). Third count, same position as first. Fourth count, same position as second. With foot extended, raise right arm forward from shoulder to a point above the head. Allow the back of the hand to drop on the head; reach in a diagonal direction with wrist extended to the right front corner of the room. Bend right knee. This changes the weight of the body to the right foot, and leaves the left leg in a diagonal position, with left arm in parallel position behind the body, on a line with the right arm which is reaching upward in a diagonal direction. This gives a diagonal reaching position from the left heel which remains on the floor, to the right wrist, across the back of the body. Hold for ten seconds, then

drop the arm as a dead weight instantly from the shoulder, while the right foot comes back to parallel standing position.

4. Left front diagonal, same as third movement, using left foot and left arm toward left corner of the room and bending left knee.

5. Right back diagonal. Extend the right foot toward the right corner of the room behind you, counting the same as in the third exercise. Raise the right arm above the head; drop back of hand to head; reach with wrist to the right back corner of the room, bending right knee, with weight of body on the right foot. This leaves the right diagonal position extended from the right wrist to the left heel, with activity across the back and the under muscles of leg and arm.

6. Left back diagonal. Same as fifth movement, using left foot and left arm, toward the left back corner of the room.

Group Two

1. Full arm circle. Beginning with the right arm hanging close to side, palm of hand next to leg, commence reaching with the middle finger all the way around from the side toward the front upward, until a full circle is described. To get the full value of this release movement, move the arm as slowly as possible constantly reaching with the middle finger as far as possible all the way around.

2. Same with left arm.

3. Same with both arms at the same time.

4. Elbow circle. Place the tips of fingers of the right hand on the right shoulder. Describe a circle with the elbow, beginning close to the body, then upward in front, all the way around toward the back and to first position. Keep the thought on the point of the elbow, reaching as far as possible during the whole movement, to hold the thought objectified apart from the body, in the same way in which we thought of the middle finger in the full arm circle.

5. Same with left elbow.

6. Same with both elbows at the same time.

Pulling Movements—without any Tension

1. Reach both hands as far in front of the body as possible, on a level with the shoulders, with thumbs upward; close hands gently, pull back lightly, keeping elbows on level with shoulders. Bring elbows as far back as possible without resistance.

2. Same activity with hands lifted as high as shoulder line, from the sides.

3. Same activity from above head, arms full length, bending the elbows toward the back when bringing the hands down. (An important point in these three positions lies in the hands and elbows being kept on a level with the shoulders throughout.)

Group Three—Waist Activitites

1. Lay right hand over Solar-Plexus (pit of stomach) just above waist line. Let body droop

slowly forward as far as possible without moving hips. This curved line from the drooping head to the waist line may be thought of as a fern curling up from the tip of the leaf, the result being that the spinal vertebrae are gently pulled apart throughout the entire length of the spinal column.

2. Lay right hand on right side at waist line; bend in same way to the right as far as possible, from drooping head to waist line.

3. Bend to left side in the same way to waist line.

4. Hands on back of hips, bend as far back as possible, with drooping head; then bend knees and bend a little farther.

After each one of these bending movements we should return to the erect position before starting the next one. This group of movements of waist line gently liberates Solar Plexus from the clutch of the diaphragm.

5. The following movements establish the release of the Solar Plexus from all muscular reactions of the diaphragm and is called the mowing exercise.

Let the body droop to the left in front, arms hanging from the shoulders loosely in parallel line. Swing arms slowly around to the right side (full length), then back over the head down to the left side. This movement allows the arms in their full swing from the shoulder, to describe as large a circle as possible. Starting down at the right side, swing across the front, over the head, and around back to the right side position; all the activity at the waist line, moving the hips as little as possible.

Group Four—Leg Activity—
Reaching and Kicking

1. Reaching. Raise the right leg directly in front, very slowly, not more than a foot, pulling the toes as far back as possible during the slow movement upward. Bring back to starting place, keeping toes pulled back. This activity liberates the muscles in the back of the leg from hip to heel.

2. Same, raising right leg directly to side, about a foot.

3. Same, raising right leg directly to the back, about a foot.

4, 5, 6. Same as above, with left leg.

7. Kicking. Raise the right knee toward the front, up to the level of the hip joint, pulling the toes back all the way. Kick vigorously toward the floor at an angle of 45 degrees, with heel, toes pulled back. This movement seems to release activity instantaneously from the right shoulder to the right heel.

8. Same, kicking out at right side.

9. Same, kicking downward and backward.

10, 11, 12. Same as above, with left leg.

N.B. Be sure to keep pulling the toes back as far as possible during the entire movements of stretching and kicking.

After having done all the foregoing movements six months, regularly, the following may be added. Always in doing any form of activity release keep the body poised over the balls of the feet, lift the chin a trifle, and do not become conscious of the chest or shoulders at any time. Watch that the bend is kept over the Solar Plexus and in hip-joints, (sciatic nerves) always with chin lifted.

Group Five

1. Stand on the balls of the feet. Let the whole body droop forward loosely. Remove tension from every joint in the body until the whole body sways forward and one almosts feels like falling. See that the shoulders hang loosely in stooping position. Now think of the spine as being the stem upon which the whole body is loosely hanging. Lift the chin until the back of the neck is loosened of all tension. Now let the head poise naturally, and imagine that you are trying to push something upward with the crown of the head. Feel the release strongly down the whole spine, but do not let the action appear in any part of the body. This is called a reaching movement, for the activity and release of the spinal column and the acceleration of circulation throughout the body. It liberates each vertebra, one from the other.

2. After doing this movement three times, then imagine that the reaching process comes from the crown of the head to the balls of the feet, along the

backs of the legs the whole length of the body, and rise slowly on tiptoe; come down to the level of the floor and rise again, with the feeling of releasing the whole body via the spinal column three times.

II

UNFOLDMENT OF INNER EAR

Preparation For Tone Work

The first part of the sounding board that we use in this System of voice work, is the posterior portion of the skull, called the inter-osseous spaces. In order that the sound-waves which start from the vibration of the vocal cords may reach their first sounding board in this region, we must see to it that all possible tension and physical sensation are removed throughout the voice and speech-producing organs.

The first place where we discover this tension and sensation in very great degree in almost everyone, is through the lower jaw muscles, which are very closely related to the tongue muscles; consequently, we must center our first thought for release on the muscles of the jaw and tongue. When the jaw and tongue are in a perfectly released condition, we find that the tip of the tongue naturally falls against the lower lip, on top of the lower teeth, letting the rest of the tongue lie on an inclined plane until the back of the tongue lies against the upper back teeth. When the tongue is thus released from tension and sensation, it becomes a conductor of resonance. The tongue will not take this position until the lower jaw is liberated. In working to liberate the jaw we must realize that it must be so released that in all movements it may work independently of the tongue, and vice versa. When the jaw is released one has the sensation that in dropping open it seems to fall toward the neck rather than being used to open the mouth. Always lift the chin a little before releasing the jaw.

Tone Work Movement No. 1

Place the tips of the first fingers against the neck under the ears. Imagine that a horizontal bar goes through the neck at this point and the head swings upon it back and forth on a pivot. Leave the neck quiet and tip the head back and forth upon the top of the neck, slowly. In tipping the head back merely think of lifting the chin. You will see that this instantaneously releases all tension and physical sensation at the back of the neck. Now swing the head forward and back as though on a pivot until the chin touches the front of the neck, then lift the chin again, etc.

Tone Work Movement No. 2

Lay both hands upon the cheeks along either side of the jaw until the finger tips touch the cheek directly over the hinge that fastens the lower jaw to the upper. Gradually release the jaw as much as possible, and in so doing press the fingers between the upper and lower jaw at the joint until you can feel the action, both when it closes consciously and when it lets go through release, as we wish it to, without any physical sensation.

The strong muscles on either side of the lower jaw that fasten it to the upper jaw (which is stationary), we may call the "chewing" muscles. The main reason for their activity is the chewing of our food, and power is used when we chew our food with these muscles. These muscles have no other reason for being used. The slight movement of the lower jaw necessary for usage in speech-sounds can be used without sensation. The wide-open mouth which has been considered necessary in producing the vocal tone of singers can be easily proven (when vocal tone is made on pure resonance), to be wholly unnecessary.

The definite delicacy of action with which we can use the speech organs, when they are independent in activity, is most amazing. There are only *seven letters* in the English alphabet that require *any* movement of the jaw, when action of the chewing muscles is laid aside in speech. We may call these the teeth sounds. When the teeth are brought together for certain letter sounds, c, g, h, j, s, x, and z, this is the only need of jaw movement in any language, and this movement is so slight that it is done without sensation.

In making a careful analysis of the reason for tension in the usage of the speech-organs in any language, we find tension to be the most evident, because of the lack of independence between the tongue and jaw movements. In most cases they seem tied together, inseparable in action. Every time the tongue is moved the jaw muscles react in tension, and vice versa.

As we work out this principle of release we find the tongue movements in all languages representing the highest proportion of speech activity. The activity of the lips is next in proportion, and the jaw the least of all. When these three speech organs, tongue, lips and jaw, are liberated to the point of independent action, there is no sensation, and a liquid flow of sound definitely and delicately adjusted to every need in any language is most gratifying to those who speak, read or sing.

Tone Work Movement No. 3

When the jaw and tongue have become so independent in their activity that with one thought they will drop into the released position, then we may begin to study the syllable sounds and their anaylsis.

In preparing the tone-producing organs and the organs of speech for the free emission of the perfectly balanced tone, we must go back to fundamental principles to find the reason for the care that must be taken in releasing these organs from all tension and sensation, nerve and muscular. We find very few people who speak with a liberated condition of the organs of speech. Consequently, it is well for us to analyze as closely as possible the condition in which we find ourselves in this regard.

The pupil who is studying this System without a teacher, should sit before a mirror in a quiet, easy position in order that he may be able to see the exact effect of the movements. The tongue, lips and jaw are the most important of the speech-producing organs, and they must be released from all sensation and tension in activity. (We use the mirror only to observe what the right position is when attained, not to watch movements).

Tone Work Movement No. 4

Close the mouth naturally and swallow. During the process of swallowing notice the position of the tongue. If one swallows naturally, the tongue rises and almost fills the roof of the mouth. Leave the tongue in this position for a few seconds. Place the first and second fingers between the upper and lower jaw on the sides of the checks so that the tips of the fingers may touch the muscles that fasten the lower jaw to the upper. Gradually drop the lower jaw away from the upper, with all the release possible, until it seems as though the lower jaw is sinking back and in this manner the mouth is opened only enough to allow the teeth to remain a half-inch apart. This position allows the tip of the tongue to operate in and out between the teeth, permitting free speech movement.

Tone Work Movement No. 5

Swallow, allowing the tongue to fill the roof of the mouth. Drop the jaw as before, and allow the tip of the tongue to find its way slowly over the top of the lower teeth until it touches the inside of the lower lip. Then proceed to drop the jaw as in Movement No. 4, leaving the back of the tongue as nearly as possible in the high position that it has taken during the act of swallowing.

Repeat this movement very slowly several times, watching carefully that there is no conscious action of the muscles of the jaw or tongue. When the jaw is actually dropped into the position that it takes when opened through released action, and the tongue is so liberated that while the tip is touching the inside of the lower lip, resting on top of the lower teeth, and the back of the tongue lies almost if not quite, against the upper back teeth—it is then that we have found the condition which liberates the jaw and tongue muscles completely from all connection and reaction with the muscles of the throat, or from the influence each may have upon the other.

In doing these movements it is well to use a slight pressure of the fingers upon the cheeks to assist the lower jaw in its separation from the upper. For if there is any conscious action of these muscles during the dropping of the jaw, it is immediately felt by the finger tips. It is also necessary before taking these movements for the liberation of jaw and tongue, to be sure there is no tension or sensation in the back of the neck. Consider for a few seconds that the head and neck are separate in their action; that the head is sitting upon the top of the neck, as it were, and that the head may swing back and forth upon the neck as though upon a pivot placed at the base of the ears.

It becomes so easy, in these days of strenuous living, to use the head and neck in their movements as though they had no individual action, that in many cases one finds a condition of tension at the top of the spine and the base of the brain. It is utterly impossible to work for the release of tongue and jaw until this condition of tension and sensation at back of the neck is removed.

When one has attained this position of the jaw and tongue, which is the result of a released condition, the tongue seems to go "uphill" from the tip to the back, which position might seem to one who did not understand, as though it would obstruct the flow of tone from the throat. No matter what position the tongue may hold in singing, if the muscles reflect any tension or sensation, that tension will be a damper to the flow of resonance. On the other hand, no matter what position the tongue may take in the production of tone, if it is without muscular tension and sensation, it *acts* as a *conductor* of resonance. To illustrate: any part of the body, when liberated from tension and sensation, is a conductor of sound-waves and resonance, from the crown of the head to the soles of the feet. That is why, through the release of all activity from tension and physical sensation, we are able to eliminate sensation in activity from the whole body. Only through *this understanding* does it become a sounding board for the voice, and thus prove the voice to be a stringed instrument.

Diction—Speech Analysis

Diction is the science of speech-sound analysis and production. It is the study of intermediate sounds through the unfoldment of the inner ear. Many teachers of singing seem to approach the study of diction merely as a matter of vocal *finish*. In *this* approach to speech and vocal sound, the study of diction is so closely related to that of tonal production that from the beginning they go hand in hand; for without perfection in the production of tone, perfect diction may not be attained, and without perfection in diction it is impossible to reach a vocal balance in any language.

Teachers of singing in Europe often praise the beauty of American voices, but always criticize the inactivity of the speech-producing organs of American students. This great fault, which has been laid at the door of the organs of speech, I find to be wholly due to the lack of the awakening of the inner ear and all the finer sensibilities. The inner ear is capable of being developed to the point of reflecting many thousands of different sounds. In the ordinary human being who has had any average culture, we find the number of sounds to which the nerves of the inner ear respond to be extremely limited in proportion to its capacity. In America most of us reach the age of maturity at least before our ear has become familiar with the sounds of more than one language. In Europe everyone becomes familiar with at least more than one language in early childhood. Thus the American student of singing, compared with the European student, appears to great disadvantage in regard to fluency of speech in song—not because of inactivity of the organs of speech, but because of lack of sensitivity of the inner ear and its application to speech sounds.

Study of the *intermediate* sounds in every language is absolutely necessary before that language may be well spoken. Audible sounds in any language are those which are clearly audible to any ear. Intermediate sounds are those sounds which we find in inflection. When the hidden sound is joined to the audible sound, the difficulty that we find in giving the proper proportion to intermediate sounds in any language may in almost all cases be traced to the lack of activity of the inner ear. There are thousands of nerves in the inner ear which are capable of response, each one to some certain sound or shade of sound, most of which remain unawakened throughout the lifetime. It is the awakening of these latent nerves and their reactions through careful sound analysis and observation, both through the hearing and the understanding, that makes it possible for the student to gain clear diction.

VOWELS

Movement No. 1

The student who is studying this System without a teacher should sit comfortably before a mirror, facing a window if possible. Take the position of the released tongue and jaw as explained in Tone Work Movement No. 1 and No. 2. Now say the sound of "A" very slowly, listening intently, allowing the jaw to remain unconscious, the tip of the tongue to lie against the lower lip over the lower teeth, and the back of the tongue to take any position necessary to make clear the sound of "A". Inflect upward a trifle in saying the sound. It is easier this way to prolong it. Listen intently—do it several times, and see if you can begin to detect the delicate joining of the two audible sounds which we find in the proper pronunciation of the long sound of "A" as used in English. The audible sounds are "A" and "E"—not long "E" exactly, but toward the "E". Only look in the mirror enough to make sure the tip of the tongue lies against the lip. Then close the eyes and slowly inflect the sound upward until the movement of the tongue, in making it clear, becomes more and more delicate and the sound becomes purer and purer. At the end of the sound of "E" the back of the tongue lies against the upper back teeth, while the tip lies over the lower front teeth against the lip.

Movement No. 2

Take same position and slowly say the sound of long "E". Here the only audible sound we find is the first, which is clearly "E_2". It is preceded, however, and ended with a slight inflection toward and from the clear "E" sound. Say it over several times until the action of the tongue becomes very gentle but decisive. In this exercise, after being sure that the jaw is released and the tongue lies against the lip on top of the lower teeth, it is best to say the sounds slowly with the eyes closed until they become perfectly clear. Then look in the glass and see the action that takes place without sensation to produce it. If we look in the mirror while the tongue muscles adjust themselves to the various sounds, we are almost sure to use conscious direction in producing them. When we close our eyes and intently listen while the tongue is adjusting itself to the sound, and the action is allowed to be without any sensation, thus we are getting spontaneous action without sensation. After we have found spontaneous action in producing each sound, it can do no harm to observe what the position is, if we are careful to keep the thought of released activity without sensation.

Movement No. 3

Analyze the sound of "I" in the same manner. Here we find three audible sounds, "Ah," "I" (long I) and "E" (long E). These sounds are connected by intermediate sounds through inflection. At first it may seem a little awkward to the student to allow the tip of the tongue to rest lightly against the lower lip during all of these movements, on top of the lower teeth, but the fact that it does seem awkward proves conclusively that there is tension in the roots of the tongue, and when that tension is removed it is in an absolutely comfortable position, without sensation. The tension and sensation may possibly be in the jaw as well as the tongue, if the tongue seems to recede from the lip, and it is well often to turn the thought to the release of the jaw and tongue muscles, for when both are released, this position of the jaw and tongue is always without sensation.

Movement No. 4

The vowel "O", to be clearly given, requires the quick movement of the lips towards closing in order that it may be finished clearly—also the vowel "U". Because of this it is easier in these beginning movements to omit the finished sounds of these two vowels and become familiar with the first sound, which may be instantaneously released. In giving this first sound of "O" and "U" it is only the starting impulse we may be able to use, just the tiniest bit of the letter that we can possibly give in a manner that we may feel that we have released it. Let go of it instantaneously without using the lips at all. "U" starts with back of tongue high as in long sound of "E" and ends by activity of lips as in "OO". It seems to inflect from "E" to "OO".

After having mastered the vowel sounds in this manner, we may take up the letters of the alphabet in their order:

"B" requires the quick closing and letting go of the lip action, and the action of the tongue that we have learned belongs to the letter "E". Those two sounds must be given instantaneously and simultaneously. "E" must always allow the tip of the tongue to remain on the lower lip, on top of the teeth.

In analyzing the consonant sounds in this manner, we find that in almost every letter of the alphabet we have some modification of the sound of "A" or "E", which gives us the most released position of the tongue that allows the tip to touch the lip, while the back of the tongue lies high against the upper back teeth.

"C" is a combination of the action of the tip of the tongue against the closed teeth and the action which brings the long sound of "E". We call any sound which brings the teeth together, a "teeth sound".

"D" requires the light touch of the tip of the tongue just behind the upper front teeth, coupled with the long sound of "E" which should always allow the tongue to lie against the lower lip.

When the lower jaw is released at the point where it is fastened to the upper jaw, it can remain so at all times in all sounds in all languages. The only time the lower jaw needs to move is when sounds are used which bring the teeth together—only seven of these in the English alphabet—C, G, H, J, S, X, Z.

"F" gives us a modification of the sound of "E" with a touch of the lower lip against the upper teeth. The more each of these sounds is prolonged, in the study of their analysis, the more awakened are the nerves of the inner ear. Consequently, slow, careful work with intense listening *only* will bring results.

"G" requires the slight action of the tongue behind the closed teeth and coupled with the sound of "E".

"H" begins with the long sound of "A" with a slight release of the tongue behind the closed teeth.

"J" is a slight action of the tongue behind the closed teeth coupled with the sound of "A".

The more delicate the action of the tongue when used against the teeth on these various sounds, the clearer the sound will become. The extreme tip of the tongue is capable of an intense activity and may be developed to the point of extreme sensitiveness in this work, if freely released and its action reduced to a minimum.

On the under side of the tip of the tongue you will see a muscle which extends its entire length. At the end of this muscle under the tip we find a nerve center which is capable of extreme sensibility when awakened to its full activity. Because of the prevailing custom of keeping the tongue *behind* the *lower teeth,* this nerve is scarcely ever functioning as it should in speech activity, for so long as it remains behind the teeth the extreme tip is curled under and this nerve, which lies just under the tip, never can become awakened to sensibility and activity. Thus we find this tip lacking in all its possibilities as the most important muscular movement in speech activity.

Thus we may understand the reason for the great

importance given to the position of the tip of the tongue always lying on top of the lower front teeth and against the lower lip at all times, when not in use. When in this position the *inside* of the lower lip and the *under side* of the tip of the tongue are together and each becomes sensitive to the touch and seeks association. As long as this association is allowed to remain we are protected from any tension or sensation in the speech organs or the muscles of the throat during activity. When the tip of the tongue lies in this position against the lower lip on top of the lower teeth, the back of the tongue should lie high against the upper back teeth, with the release of the lower jaw, as we have previously explained it. In looking at this position of tongue and jaw in a mirror, the teeth are apart a half an inch and the tongue is on an inclined plane, to the upper back teeth.

"K" is to be done with a slight touch of the back of the tongue preceding the position for the long sound of the vowel "A".

"L" starts with the back of the tongue high, as in the syllable "Eh", and ends with the tip touching just back of the upper front teeth.

"M" starts with the back of the tongue high, as in the sound of the syllable "Eh", and ends with the lips coming together.

"N" starts the same as "M" but ends with the tip of the tongue touching behind the upper front teeth.

"P" starts with the lips touching together and

ends with the position of the long sound for the vowel "E".

"Q" starts with the back of the tongue touching the roof of the mouth and ends with the position for the vowel "U" with the activity of both lips at end, of "OO".

"R" starts with the position of "Ah" and ends by raising the tip of the tongue toward upper front teeth.

"S" starts with position of "Eh", and ends with the tip of the tongue making a soft hiss back of closed teeth.

"T" starts with touch of tongue back of upper teeth and ends with position of long sound of "E".

"V" starts with the lower lip against upper front teeth and ends with position of long "E".

"W" starts with touch of tongue as for "D", next through modification of "U" to sound of "B" by touching lips together, next modification of "U" again, followed by tongue behind upper front teeth as for "L" and ends with position for vowel "U".

"X" starts with position of "Eh", and ends in position of "S" with teeth together.

"Y" starts with position of vowel "I" preceded with quick opening of lips.

"Z" starts with position of hard hissing sound against the teeth and ends with position of vowel "E".

N.B. A deeper understanding and a clearer analysis of the sounds of the English alphabet may be found in the first part of this book, in Essay entitled, "Speech Analysis". This essay gives a grouping and condensation of the alphabet which is most valuable.

III
FOUNDATION OF RESONANCE
(Vocalises—Panofka)

Vocal resonance is entirely dependent on the blending of two conditions which are known acoustically as upper and lower overtones. The upper overtones were intended to furnish all the carrying power necessary for any usage of the voice, and the source of upper overtones is the elemental sounding board (which is known as the inter-osseous spaces across the back of the skull). These upper overtones adequately supply all needs of the child voice up to the age of adolescence. From this period the lower overtones, which furnish color and richness (emotional content), begin to blend with the upper overtones, and from thence supply depth and beauty as long as we live. *This* condition if *understood* and *protected* from birth, would bring into every voice a state of *natural* tuning; but unfortunately, the value of the upper overtones has in no way been understood or applied, and only the few great voices in every generation are found to have this state of natural tuning.

In this System, we begin by restoring this child condition of upper overtones to every voice. In so doing we use what we call "squeals" first of all, to awaken the inter-osseous spaces (elemental sounding board) of the head to the reflection of sound-waves, and they should be started on pitches at least four tones—the more the better—above the highest pitch in the voice upon which a singing tone has been produced. The vowel used in producing these "squeals" is "eh" as in the word, "met", leaving off the "m" and "t".

The reasons for starting the "squeals" so far above ordinary singing pitches are many. First of all, we wish to produce an entirely distinct condition different in every way from any vocal condition before experienced. Vocal tone production as it is usually given, depends upon frontal resonance and breath support. Any tone that is dependent upon the support of the breath, however well controlled physically, is utterly incapable of becoming a perfectly balanced tone in the tuned state of resonance alone; for the very pressure of the breath from below, however slight, brings a reaction in the resistance of the muscles and nerves surrounding the larynx and controlling the pharynx, which entirely shuts off the possibility of using the elemental sounding board. Consequently, the vocal tone as we usually find it, being dependent upon breath support and frontal resonance, is produced almost entirely through the medium of lower overtones. *This means* that while the middle and possibly the lower tones of the compass may sound well and appear balanced, whatever upper pitches may be included in the compass are the result of the lower overtones being pushed from below by the breath support, instead of having been reflected from the elemental sounding board which is the primal source of upper overtones.

That is the reason that all voices used from the "old" viewpoint are almost always limited as to compass and power, if not quality. For instance most sopranos have a very definite feeling of limit around upper "G" or "A", the same as most tenors; while contraltos and bass voices find their limit around low "C" and "A". I consider that this sense of limitation at either end of any voice is due, first of all, to its being used out of place (balance), for the moment any tone in any voice comes as a result of the balance and blending between upper and lower overtones, that tone immediately gives the sensation of being in a speaking voice condition, no matter upon what pitch it may be given.

The ideal state of the singing voice is that condition which gives the sensation, that one has only to speak in the natural manner of speaking and this sound will be instantly reflected to any pitch within the whole compass, whether that compass extends throughout two or three octaves, and that speaking instantly brings the clear, ringing, full, rich, singing tone, with no more physical effort than we use in our ordinary conversational voice. The only physical sensation which should come in any part of the singing voice as a result of producing a singing tone, is the sensation of resonance, which is reflected sound-waves and never within the cavities of head or throat.

In the first stage of building, this sensation seems to be outside, reflected from the elemental sounding board, afterwards expanding in all directions; it also follows the sensation of the resonance flowing down the spine, across the shoulders and chest, and thence downward through the whole body, last of all the feet.

When fully established, the resonated condition may be easily felt by laying the hand on any part of the body, in the same manner that we feel the resonance when we lay the hand on the sounding board of a piano. When the singer sings in this completely tuned condition, he feels that the voice is all resonance and he is playing upon it with his thought, in space, outside and apart from the body.

It follows then that in establishing this new condition in any and every voice, we must first use the thin, shrill sounds which we call "squeals", and which are the result of awakening the activity of the elemental sounding board—the primal source of upper overtones. This gives everyone first of all the sensation of producing sound—noise—entirely away from the aid or influence of the breath, and in such a manner that the throat and the whole vocal area are left entirely without sensation in its production.

In producing the squeals, first of all we should entirely free the mind from making a sound in any way musical, for since we are using only half the condition necessary to produce a musical tone, we cannot possibly expect it to result in a sound in any way pleasing to the ear. The farther our thought can be taken away from the singing voice as such in producing these noises or "squeals", the better results we will get in this phase of the work. Think of the shrill cry of a very young babe, or the squeal of a little pig, or the peep of a bird, or the shrill bleat of a little lamb, or even the squeak of a rat—any of these little, shrill, piercing sounds of nature will give us a far better idea for the producing of sound entirely through upper overtones than any thought of a singing tone.

Next, sit before a mirror, find the unconscious position for jaw and tongue which has been described several times previously, and then gently say the syllable "eh" exactly as though you were saying the word "met" leaving off the sound of the "m" and "t". Study to give exactly the same sound that is found in the word "met" with an instantaneous release of speaking.

There are various slight changes which may be made in the sound which take us away from the best results in producing these "squeals". If a singer has found, we will say, upper "A" as being the limit of the singing voice, prepare the unconscious position, think of releasing the sound of "eh", with the instantaneous impulse which we have used in releasing the syllable sounds, and touch upon the piano E flat above high C several times. The first impression is that it is utterly impossible to make even a sound upon this pitch. That is because our thought has been entirely taken up previously with the attempt to make musical sounds upon all pitches.

When we entirely drop our responsibility of making musical sounds and try to realize the thinnest, ugliest, shrillest noise possible, we begin to see that we can produce that kind of an elemental sound upon this extreme pitch. We cannot do it, however, with the slightest preparation of the breath. If it seems necessary to take a breath because of old habits, just before we release this squeal, stop a second and let the breath out, then before we take another, give this sound of "eh" a spoken release.

Gradually, as we try mentally, not physically, in this way, thinking of the piercing noise, getting farther and farther away from the old thought of tone production, it will dawn upon our consciousness that these upper pitches have a sound which belongs to them alone, as much as any of the lower pitches which we have formerly used have the musical tone which belongs to them. Sometimes it is possible to get the direct imitation of some nature sound. There are many ways of approaching this condition and different ways appeal to different people. You are perfectly safe in experimenting if you remember that no sensation in any part of the head, throat, or body may accompany the production of these "squeals"—upper overtones.

In producing "squeals" it is well to go so slowly that each sound is entirely separate in the thought from each of the other sounds. Only in this manner do we get absolute freedom and spontaneity. It is best also not to devote more than ten minutes at any time to the using of these noises. Also observe closely whether the muscles in the back of the neck are kept absolutely released, for the tension upon these nerves and muscles directly dampers the resonance in all or any of the elementary reflecting conditions.

In men's voices, whether they are bass or tenor, we can always approach the "squeals" quite easily through the thought of falsetto. So-called falsetto tones in a man's voice are really what is left of the child voice before adolescence, and used in a manner we call enclosed. In other words, a falsetto tone can never become legitimate from the old viewpoint of breath and its control. At the age of adolescence a boy's voice drops an octave in timbre. From this time, only a very few men's voices partake of upper overtones to any degree. This is why, if the higher pitches are needed, the vocal condition readjusts to that of the child voice, and pitches may be used which are called falsetto. In this System of voice production, this whole upper octave of the man's voice which can be used as falsetto, may be liberated into a state of perfect tuning and become legitimate tones at any age.

I find that it is best, after the first few "squeals" have been produced in a manner that is fairly satisfactory, to use the arpeggio of the scale in the following manner: 8, 5, 3, 1. We will say the first squeal is on "F" above high "C", the next squeal upon "C", the next "A" and then "F", each group comprising an octave. The temptation after squealing upon the first pitch and taking the next "squeal" on the next pitch below, is to readjust in a degree at least the muscular condition; for we all for so many years have felt it necessary to make a new, conscious adjustment of throat muscles for each pitch, that it is a little difficult at first to realize that whatever muscular adjustment is necessary will be done without any sensation, if we keep our thought entirely away from the *change* of pitch, as we take the different pitches. So, imagine in taking each arpeggio that we are taking a natural speaking sound, that is, that all tones and pitches are the result of a natural speaking condition of release. While we are thinking this consciously, if we are touching the different tones on the keyboard as we produce the "squeals", we will soon see that we are getting away from all conscious muscular adjustment, and in this manner of doing the inner ear is directing the voice to follow the pitches given from the keyboard spontaneously, without sensation (via reflection), instead of by the conscious direction of the outer ear, which is the physical ear and demands conscious adjustment of muscles for every pitch and tone, with physical sensation on every sound.

When we allow the inner ear to direct, our consciously directed thought is entirely taken up with the thought of each group of four tones being given in a natural condition of speech. This is our first step in approaching the use of the "double consciousness" (so-called) which results in all physical action being spontaneous action, for any action resulting from the direction of the will power is always conscious action. Spontaneous action is physically sensationless. In getting at this result, we continually direct the voice through the use of the keyboard until we have reached the point where all muscular adjustment and readjustment has been laid aside in producing tone, pitch or word.

Our intention is first of all to take away the old fear of extreme pitches, whether high or low, but in order to make possible the production of extremely low pitches in any voice, we have first to establish the free emission of sounds made upon extremely *high* pitches, entirely through upper overtones. In order to bring about the free production of the lowest sound possible for bass or contralto voices, we have *first* to establish the spontaneous release of the *upper* overtones through the squeals on extremely *high* pitches, exactly in the same manner that we work them out for the soprano and tenor voices. This may seem a little difficult to understand at this point of the work, but it will be explained in many other ways later.

When we have reached this place in our understanding of elemental sounds (the upper overtones), and they can be produced easily over a compass of two or three octaves with the sound of "eh", we have really adjusted the whole voice in its production from end to end with its instantaneous reflection from the elemental sounding board. Our next step makes clear the manner in which the *lower* overtones may also be reflected from the elemental sounding board throughout this compass, through a very gradual blending with the upper overtones in every pitch. In order to adjust this gradual blending of the *two* sets of overtones in *every* pitch, we must use the initial sound of the vowel *"O"*. This *beginning* sound of "O" does *not* use the movement of the lips. (It is the ending of the sound that brings the simultaneous use of both lips). If in the *every-day* use of the *speaking voice* everyone *naturally* used a tuned condition, this adjustment of the upper and lower overtones that we are making throughout the voice would be quite a simple matter. But only one mature voice in thousands uses a tuned condition for speech sounds. This is because the basic value of the *preservation* of upper overtones *from birth* to adolescence in all voices had not been known. When we accept the fact that the motive power of the human voice, for singing as well as speaking, is adequately supplied through the understanding and protection of the use of the elemental sounding board which is the *source* of *upper* overtones, all physical effort and sensation in its production can be laid aside.

We should begin making the vowel "O" across the center voice one tone at a time back and forth through the intervals of thirds, fifths and octaves. From this point little melodies can be followed and higher and lower notes added, until gradually throughout the whole compass the blending of the upper and lower overtones in each pitch is perfected. After having worked for a period of time—the length depends entirely upon the condition of the individual voice—we should take up the study of Panofka, Opus 85, Book I, with all voices. We begin by using two measures at a time with the syllable vowel sound of "O", released in exactly the same manner that we use it for the squeals.

If possible, the person who is studying should sit or stand away from the keyboard, not even looking at it or the notes, while someone plays the melody of the exercise two measures at a time. The thought of the singer should be that of releasing a sound with "O" and allowing it to flow continuously from a spoken condition, away from the lips, for a few seconds. His conscious thought should be wholly occupied with his interest in the sound remaining in a speech condition while it proceeds from him. During this time, the person at the piano should play the first two measures of the first exercise, fairly rapidly.

The singer's voice at first will blur over these pitches from the first to the last, because no conscious muscular adjustment is used. He should be trying *not* to hear the pitches of the piano consciously with the "*outer* ear". His "*inner* ear" *will hear them* and direct his voice so that it will follow the tones, at first in a blur, and gradually as his release becomes more perfect, in clearer and clearer tones on each pitch *without* muscular adjustment. This feeling establishes spontaneous action for readjustment and at the same time allows the singer to get the consciousness of a unity from the beginning of the first measure to the end of the second, which results in the full realization that his tone is outside of himself, flowing from a speech condition on expansion, entirely away from the old thought of high and low pitch.

Each exercise in this book should be so taken, with great care and patience, and only a few minutes at any one time. This work requires the complete unfoldment of a vision of analysis, which keeps the interest of the conscious and outer ear associated with the speech condition of release and flowing sound, entirely apart from physical sensation and will power direction.

Through this means of liberation, the inner ear and all the finer sensibilities are allowed to take charge of the production of sound and speech, and to keep them *entirely disassociated* from physical sensation while they are unfolding into a perfection of musicianship and tonal beauty which gradually becomes spontaneously unlimited in all directions.

IV

BASIC UNDERSTANDING FOR VOCAL WORK

(Vocalises—Vaccai)

An impulse of any syllable is the least possible sound of that syllable that we can let go of instantly, and in so doing drop the jaw and tongue to the unconscious position. This release of the first impulse of a syllable is a matter entirely of mental concept. The process has to be thought over and analyzed many times before the student can get a clear idea of what is desired. We are entirely dependent upon the correct usage of this initial sound of every syllable and its instantaneous release, for not only the clarity of the syllable itself, but also the beginning of the perfectly tuned vocal tone.

This first syllable, in the first exercise of "Vaccai", "Man", would seem to be, when analyzed, merely a "Ma" (as in "Ah"). However, if our thought is of "Ma" without the thought of instantaneous release, our mind is holding the positive form of the "Ah" sound to the very end of the tone. The release of the impulse "Ma" gives us the sound of "Ma" in a fraction of a second. This definite little touch that comes with the release of the initial sound in this way, corresponds in its action upon the vocal cords to the tips of the finger upon the string of the harp. In reality, it is this little quick release which liberates the sound-waves in such a way that there is no physical sensation whatsoever in their beginning, and leaves all of the resonating conditions absolutely free from any tension or sensation in order that they may reflect the sound-waves perfectly. The second impulse of any syllable will always come in clearly, without conscious thought applied, in proportion as the first impulse is released and detached—that is, the more instantaneously the thought releases the initial sound of any syllable, the more freely will the speech activity bring in the various sounds of the second impulse without sensation and instantaneously.

If the thought and inner ear, and tongue and jaw, have been carefully and thoughtfully adjusted to all of the sounds in the letter analysis as previously given, they will respond spontaneously to all the intermediate sounds in the second impulse of any syllable without conscious thought or direction. Hence, we find that conscious thought is applied only in the direct instantaneous release of the first impulse of each syllable, one after the other. As quickly as we have released the first impulse of one syllable, our thought should instantly fly to the thought of the release of the next syllable, and the next, and so on. This keeps conscious thought wholly taken up with the consecutive release of the first impulse of each syllable, and allows the second impulse of each syllable to come in spontaneously with no conscious thought.

This instantaneous adjustment of the thought from one first impulse to the next, leaving a second or two between (in which the sound-waves reflect), gives a completeness and a continuity to each sentence which is entirely necessary when we reach the stage of interpretation, allowing each set of sound waves when liberated to overlap the preceding one. This overlapping of the sound-waves gives the stringed instrument its legato.

It is well to go over the first impulse of each syllable in this exercise many times, just using simple conversational tone, and not considering the pitches in any way. After the thought has been clearly established in this manner, it is ample time to touch the key on the keyboard of the piano, allowing the voice to follow the leading of the one who plays. The impulse of each syllable should be done in as sensationless a condition as possible, with the feeling that the speech condition and sound of the speaking voice are preserved, no matter where upon the keyboard, in the scale, or on the staff the pitches may appear.

As a result of the work in letter analysis which the student has previously done, we now take it for granted that the spontaneous movements of the tongue, lips and jaw, without sensation, will produce combinations of sounds instantaneously and simultaneously until the idea has been perfectly and clearly established.

In the second syllable of the first exercise in "Vaccai", we have the combination of "C" and "A" given with the same sound of "A". The third syllable has the combination of "S" with the "O". "O" is one of the most difficult vowels to release, for the first sound of "O" starts with the slightest movement on the top at the back of the tongue, with no lip movement whatever. The *first impulse* of "O" does *not* sound like the "O" we are used to hearing. It is only the beginning of "O", which proves that most of the "O" sound is dependent upon the lip action, which comes entirely in the second impulse. So the third syllable is an instantaneous release of the "S" coupled with the first sound of "O", which is a long way from being the finished sound of "O" as we are used to hearing it instantly given.

It is this careful taking apart of the intermediate sounds of letters through which we are able to develop the response of the latent nerves of the inner ear, and through them in time we become able to distinguish shades of sound which at first we were incapable of hearing at all.

The next syllable is "Le" ("A" as in "Hay"). "A" must be released with its initial sound, which is not by any means the entire sound of the letter "A". We have learned in the letter analysis that the long sound of "A" is a combination of two sounds, consequently the release of the "L" coupled with the first sound of "A" is what we want. The remaining inflection sounds of "A" combined, from the second impulse of this syllable, should come spontaneously.

The next syllable is "Ci" which in its entirety is

pronounced like "Che" in "Cheat". Here again we must release the sound of the "Ch" coupled with the initial sound of the "E", which is the first of the two sounds of the complete "E", leaving the pure "E" sound to come as a second impulse. The last syllable of this sentence is the combination of "T" with the sound of "A" as in "Ah".

We will now take up the second sentence in "Vaccai"—Piu, de, lu, sa, to". The first impulse of the first syllable, "Piu", we release with the sound of "P" coupled with the first impulse of the sound of "U". The first impulse of the sound of "U" does not get clearly into the "U" sound. The second impulse of the sound of "U" is made with the lips; the first impulse with a little movement of the back of the tongue. "U" and "Q" are difficult sounds to release, because we have never been taught before to separate the first from the second sound.

The second syllable is released with the sound of "D" made with the tip of the tongue just behind the upper front teeth, coupled with the long sound of "A", but only the first impulse of the sound of "A". The third syllable is released with the sound of "L" coupled with the first impulse of the sound of "U", exactly the same sound of "U" that we find in the first syllable of the second sentence. The next syllable is released with the sound of "S" softened slightly. In Italian, some sounds of "S" and "Z" are coupled slightly with the sound of "T"-"Z", with a much clearer sound of "T" than "S", as in Mezzo Soprano, that is commonly used. Here the

"T" is plainly audible. The fourth syllable of the second sentence of this exercise, then, we find released with a soft sound of "S" as in our word "so" and the broad sound of "A". The last syllable is released with the sound of "T" coupled with the first impulse of the sound of "O".

The third sentence of this exercise is released with the broad sound of "A" as in "Ah", coupled with the sound of "E" made by touching the tip of the tongue behind the upper front teeth. The second syllable is released with the sound of "C" coupled with the first impulse of "O". The third syllable, "Che", pronounced like the letter "K", is released with the first impulse of the sound of the letter "K" which takes in the first impulse of the long sound of "A". The fourth syllable "Sa" is analyzed in the preceding sentence. The fifth syllable is released with the soft sound of "C" coupled with the first impulse of the sound of the letter "E". The last syllable is released with the sound of the letter "T" and the first impulse of the sound of the letter "E".

In the fourth sentence, the first syllable is the letter "C" coupled with the first impulse of "O". In the second syllable of this sentence, "Lie", we find two vowel sounds to be released consecutively. The "L" is released coupled with the first impulse of the letter "I", to which is added the first impulse of the letter "A" pronounced like the "e" in our English word, "met". The third syllable, release the sound of "V" coupled with the first impulse of "A" as "e" in "met". Fourth syllable, release "F" coupled with the first impulse of "I" followed by first impulse of "A" as in "met". Last syllable, release "T" with the first impulse of "O".

Fifth sentence, release "F" with the first impulse of "A" (broad sound). Second syllable "Ce" (pronounced "che") as "e" in "met". Third syllable "Che" (pronounced like "K"), coupled with the first impulse of the sound of "E", which in Italian is like "e" in "met". Fourth syllable, release "P" coupled with impulse of broad sound of "A". Fifth syllable "Pi", release "P" coupled with the first impulse of the sound of "E". Last syllable, release "T" coupled with the first impulse of broad sound of "A".

Sixth sentence, release "P" coupled with first impulse of "R". Second syllable, release "S" coupled with the first impulse of "O", followed by first impulse of "A" (broad sound). Third syllable, release "M" coupled with first impulse of "O". Fourth syllable, release "R" coupled with first impulse of sound of "E" like "e" in "met". The last two sentences are the 5th and 6th sentences repeated.

Note: In this volume of Vaccai is found an analysis of the sounds of the Italian language.

In taking up the exercises in "Vaccai", it is well to understand the purpose of the book to some extent. This book of vocalises takes in every principle of embellishment that finds its place in vocal music. Each exercise also is graded, from the complete diatonic scale which we find in the first exercise, through each interval of that scale to the octave. Each exercise emphasizes and makes familiar the use of some particular interval. From the standpoint of musicianship, this affords the student most excellent ear training for the inner ear, in establishing to an absolute certainty each interval of the diatonic scale in the consciousness. I believe we can trace the faulty singing of intervals and embellishments to the same cause to which we trace faulty diction—to the lack of awakening and sensitizing the activity of the inner ear. If "Vaccai" is taken up by the pupil of singing in his elementary work, and each exercise makes a clear impression on the consciousness of the student, this knowledge may be used in every stage of his unfoldment to the best possible advantage.

The mechanized daily practice by students of singing of any set of vocalises, while it may for the time being delude him into the feeling that he is progressing vocally through the completion of various books of vocal exercises, cannot possibly result in a lasting benefit to the voice; for the understanding of the scales and intervals, in the development of true musicianship, should come not through the daily grind upon the vocal organs, but through the intelligent unfoldment of understanding and the use of the inner ear activity. One great advantage of the study of "Vaccai" is the logical progression of the exercises and, most of all, its condensation of values.

To go back for a moment to the release of the tongue, jaw and lip action in the enunciation of different sounds, I wish again to lay special stress upon the point of independent action of the tongue. We find in almost every student at the beginning of the study of diction, that the three speech organs are not independent in action, one of the other. This tendency of not separating the tongue action from the action of the jaw comes from its not having been understood that each of the speech organs should act independently. The jaw and tongue have *never* been entirely separated in their activity until in this System of study; and when the jaw, tongue and lips are independent and sensationless, we are able to perfect diction as never before. When the jaw is actually released in the sensationless position that I have explained previously, then insist upon the tongue acting independently in forming all of the sounds of the alphabet, almost to the point of exaggeration, in order that the sympathy which exists between tongue and jaw in a state of tension may be eliminated.

The following is the suggested order the exercises in Vaccai should be used.

Exercise	No.	1	Page	3
"	"	2	"	4
"	"	3	"	6
"	"	4	"	9
"	"	5	"	13
"	"	6	"	18
"	"	7	"	20
"	"	8	"	22

V

LEARNING A LANGUAGE OF IMPULSES

Song Study

After having clearly established in consciousness the understanding of each sound used being reflected from the elemental sounding board, we may then approach songs in a manner which leads to the correct singing of them. Many times when a pupil seems to have established all these conditions perfectly and then takes up the study of *songs,* he will feel at first confronted by many old conditions which seemed to have been completely laid aside in the doing of the exercises.

In a song we have first of all an impression of melody, which to the thought trained in the *old* way, insists at once upon a legato (which in the old thought means a conscious physical sustaining of the breath throughout the phrase). This is the most difficult of all the sensations (which come with the thought of "singing a song") to eradicate, and sometimes seems to confront the student for months on his approach to a song.

The reason this condition makes such stubborn resistance is that our thought has been trained for so many hundreds of years to be wholly dependent upon the support of the breath, in order that our tones may seem to keep perfectly smooth in passing from one word to another. Of course, after having for months liberated the thought and action to release each syllable of every word absolutely independent one of the other, it would seem as though it should be an easy matter to apply this principle as readily to a song as to an exercise.

This point of the work is a crucial test of whether the pupil has thoroughly mastered the idea of resonance doing the work in place of the breath. If resonance is allowed to do its work without interference, it is possible for each impulse, when it is detached, to produce a set of sound waves; but in order that this may be so we not only have to let go physically the initial sound contained in each syllable instantaneously, but it must be done *mentally* as well. The explanation, first of the physical, and second of the mental, release will be illustrated later.

When the physical and mental release is simultaneous and instantaneous, the initial sound of each syllable is instantly detached. This instantaneous sound of the speaking voice is emitted through the lips with the exact spontaneity we use in speech. This speech sound plucks the vocal cords, liberating a set of sound waves which instantly travels to the elemental sounding board and is reflected into space as resonance.

This natural impulse of speaking is *never* associated with *any* pitch, but remains in the realm of the spoken sentence emitted through the lips; consequently, when each set of sound waves leaves the vocal chords, it is wholly free (when it reflects from the sounding board) to take in, blend and reflect both the upper and the lower overtones at the same instant that the reflection takes place.

As the phrase is thus given, using the language of impulses instantly detached, each set of sound-waves leaving the sounding board is thus entirely independent of the one preceding and the one following, and each one is thus able to take in the upper and lower overtones simultaneously at the point of reflection and to expand into space exactly as does the tone of the stringed instrument, each one following and overlapping the preceding one, which gives the perfect legato of the stringed instrument. There *never* comes a time (in producing tone in singing in *this* manner) when the singer himself is conscious of the condition of legato that he *always* feels in the *old* manner of sustaining the tones with the breath. Many times students will say, "Must I always feel that my work is so choppy?"; which shows that they are unconsciously holding the thought that, sooner or later, they will be able to apply all this preliminary process to the singing sensations they have felt in singing in the *old* way.

This is as impossible as the mingling of oil and water, and the sooner it can be made clear to the pupil that it is *only* through *this* sensation (of releasing each syllable absolutely separate in thought and action from the one which precedes or follows) that satisfactory results will ever be gained in this "new way" of voice production. As long as we hold in thought one fraction of responsibility from one tone to the next, just so long are we hanging in balance between the old thought and the new, and we cannot expect to feel the support which comes from free, flowing, unobstructed sound-waves as long as we in any way cling to the feeling of the consciousness of breath.

When the body is used as a sounding board or reflector, we must know that we cannot allow any physical or mental obstruction to interfere with the flow and reflection of the sound-waves throughout and from the sounding board. As long as our responsibility rests only with the release of one sound at a time, we may be sure there is no tension in any part of the body which may act as a damper to the flow of resonance.

The student who is following these directions must first of all be patient. As long as we make one move in any direction which is not dependent upon the natural impulse and spontaneity, just that moment do we begin to enter the field of artificiality, which is the greatest enemy of spontaneity. The student must also realize that the more closely each tone attains its condition of balance (the result of blending of upper and lower overtones) the more easily will he find it possible to attain the instantaneous release of the tone.

We are taking up each one of these principles in order that we may become familiar with it *long before* any part of the voice is perfectly balanced tonally. Consequently, as we do these exercises thoughtfully and slowly, and results possibly seem a little vague, it will be a comfort to know that through all these different viewpoints we are slowly and surely attaining the vocal balance which in time allows the perfect release of each impulse, followed by its perfect set of sound-waves, which will as perfectly overlap the set which precedes and follows it, and can result in no other way than the absolute legato which is and should be the goal of every student of singing, and is the legato of the "stringed" instrument, conceded to be the most perfect legato expressed in music.

The only possible way through which we may use the vocal tone based on the principle of a stringed instrument, is through the association of syllable sounds with the tonal sound from the standpoint of the impulse. In this manner the syllable sound and tonal sound are left wholly independent one of the other, as must be done to allow the instantaneous plucking of the string through which each set of sound-waves is wholly liberated from the one preceding and the one following.

When the student has thus mastered the instantaneous *release* of the *vocal* sound, through the instantaneous *detachment* of the initial sound of each syllable, he will find he is able without difficulty to apply this understanding to the sentence in a song. The application of these principles to a song is the opportunity for the student to decide just how far he will be able at this point to make his work practical. It is best always, for the first few months, to choose songs in which most of the melody, and especially at the beginning of the song, lies directly within the compass of conversational sounds. (We classify this material as "talking" songs). This applies to all voices alike. Also a song in which each syllable takes up one tone only. It is, however, just as essential that in a soprano or tenor voice, occasional excursions be made into the highest register, the voice not remaining there, however, for any considerable length of time. With a bass or contralto voice, it is just as necessary that occasionally the melody lead them into their extreme lower pitches, and not remaining away from the middle voice for any long period. The value of working for a considerable time in the middle voice in song work for all voices, is that in so doing we encounter fewer problems. A very excellent song for all voices to begin with is, "Until You Came", by Metcalf.

For temperamental students it is difficult, even in working technically with a song, to keep the thought from the import of the words. In this *beginning* work in a song, it is just as essential to keep the thought *wholly* upon the purely *technical* side as it will be later to keep the thought *wholly* upon the ideas of *interpretation.* No student, however proficient or talented, should attempt to handle these *two sides* of song work simultaneously at the beginning. If this be done, one or the other is sure to become limited, for upon one *following the other* should the whole attention be placed, and only when every technical difficulty is out of the way should students allow themselves to be wholly saturated with the atmosphere of the song.

We will then look at the technical difficulties of a song first. The first phrase of "Until You Came", —"Chill twilight hovered o'er the world"—we find given on one pitch. At a glance it would seem as though to give a fresh impulse on each of these syllables, one after the other, because they are on the same pitch, would be exceedingly easy. On the contrary, the fact is evident very soon that it is easy to become careless in releasing impulses on repeated pitches, especially in the middle voice. This sort of phrase partakes considerably of the style of the recitative, and many years ago Lamperti said that "he who has mastered the art of recitative may consider himself an artist". The art of recitative is the ability to produce all the beauty of the *singing* tone through the condition of the *spoken* sentence, and means that a perfectly balanced tonal condition must have been established *before* this becomes possible *throughout* the entire compass.

First of all, commit the words of the song to memory, so one follows the other in mind without a conscious thought. Then analyze each syllable, speaking aloud, until the mind clearly grasps all the sounds, audible and hidden, and all the inflections contained in each word. Then study the first impulse of each syllable, saying them over in the spoken voice one after the other, leaving the second impulse of each syllable entirely out of the thought.

This plan of study gives the following order of procedure:

First, committing the words to memory.

Second, analyzing each syllable carefully, speaking aloud both impulses (first and second) in each syllable.

Third, making a study of the first impulse of each syllable, until the mind instantly goes from one first impulse to the next first impulse without a conscious thought of the second impulse.

It is absolutely necessary to establish the mental attitude toward all words because this attitude *allows* an *uninterrupted* flow of the sound-wave through the phrase.

To sum up the results of this manner of approach is to realize that we must make for ourselves a *new language*—a language of impulses rather than syllables and words, so that any sentence we may read may appear to us at a glance as a sentence of first impulses, clearly impressed upon the mind.

When any foreign language is being studied, its mastery is proven only when the student is able to *think his thoughts* in the new language. When a student of *this System* can *think* his thoughts in the *language of first impulses,* he is then able to sing for the remainder of his career and keep all conditions in perfect release and balance.

VI

ADJUSTING THE VOCAL STRUCTURAL CONDITION

Fundamental Principles

In this chapter, I wish to emphasize the fact very strongly that the work covered in these chapters is really work that requires, when done with a teacher, three or four years of study.

It is well to define here the difference between a rule and a principle. A rule is something that can be learned and is only valuable for a certain length of time; a principle is a basic idea which is found to be of equal value at the completion as at the beginning—fundamental and final. A principle is something that we must recognize from the beginning to the end of our work, and is equally valuable every step of the way. Each one of these points that we take up and try to define clearly extends from the beginning to the end of our work, according to the needs of the pupil and the judgment of his teacher. Each point that is studied is essential to the full and complete unfoldment of the voice, and if correctly done need never be undone. Each section of the work that we do is essential to building and extends from the beginning to the end. We do not use rules like a series of scaffoldings to be taken apart and thrown away at each stage of development, but principles which become an *integral part of the finished structure.*

In the old way of working with the voice, it often seemed that a pupil's progress was based on the *number* of vocalises he had mastered. In *this way,* different degrees of unfoldment of the voice itself denote the progress. Each tone of the voice is tuned individually from the beginning, and yet the relationship of each tone to the unity of the whole structure is never lost sight of.

We recognize the fact that *beauty of tone* should be the end and aim of every student in vocal work, and yet we also know that *without* a *structural* condition which results in balance, dependable tonal beauty is impossible; consequently, it is far better at the beginning to have the pupil understand this perfectly—that not until the structural condition is attained is it worth while to expect beauty of tone until he has attained this balance.

Every one who works with ear training should understand that the *awakening* and usage of the *inner* ear is most essential, and the *possibilities* in the unfoldment of the inner ear seem almost *unlimited.* People who are so-called "temperamental" and have great musical feeling naturally have a highly sensitized inner ear. Nowadays, it is commonly accepted that anyone who expects to make a success in music study in any line should first have a thorough course in ear training. Ear training, adequately done, means that the *inner* ear undergoes a process of unfoldment which awakens its *latent* possibilities.

We can prove that the inner ear can be more definitely awakened, and more thoroughly attuned, through the association of resonance (which is the result of the unobstructed reflection of sound-waves) than in *any other* way, since the building of the voice in this manner of working is dependent *wholly* upon release and tuning of resonance capacity. I feel that to awaken the inner ear is a very easy matter, when it is worked out from the standpoint of carefully analyzing letter and syllable sounds associated with resonance and their relationship to the production of vocal tone, through which we find a very consistent and logical unfoldment.

A thorough understanding of resonance and its phenomena *must* come through the hearing of the *inner* ear. In recognition of this fact, I am willing to make a specific statement: if the voice is understood from the standpoint of these principles, it is possible to unfold a voice from the beginning to the end without the pupil listening to *one* tone with the *outer* ear any time, and to come into recognition of beautiful tones instantaneously *because* of the fine sensibility of the *inner* ear. I am dwelling upon this fact with great emphasis because, at the beginning, every pupil is most likely to listen for tonal beauty with the outer ear—and there is a reason for so doing—and expect to find it, unless he has been taught *not* to look for it.

It is impossible to awaken the inner ear through the recognition of resonance until one is able to use the vocal organs with perfect spontaneity and sensationless activity. In other words, we must lay aside conscious physical action and muscular adjustment *entirely* before the vocal organs are used with sensationless activity, and until this is accomplished it is impossible to gain a recognition of resonance, through which we may attune the inner ear. That is the reason why, at the very beginning of this work in the first chapter, I laid much emphasis upon the adjustment of a normal body through the release of all muscular activity from sensation and conscious will power direction.

It is impossible for the body to perform any act spontaneously, until a certain activity release has been gained which puts it in a normal condition. When every activity of the body is spontaneous and without sensation we will find there is no tension connected with any movement, and consequently, *that* movement will reflect no strain or fatigue—there is no resistance.

If the student wishes to make the most of himself in every way, mentally and vocally, he will go through the movements for released activity every day of his life. It requires only ten or fifteen minutes a day to do so, and the ultimate result is spontaneous activity apart from sensation, which brings a perfection of poise and balance under any and all circumstances.

Clear enunciation in singing is conceded by every one to be essential, and we all know that true artistic singing is not complete without it; yet very few teachers of singing place any importance upon the study of diction until a pupil has reached the realm of finish in his work. According to *this* System of vocal production, liberation and unfoldment, the formation of the word sounds and the production of tones are so closely related that it is impossible to understand one without understanding the other. From the *beginning* of the work, the two should be developed along parallel lines. In analyzing the production of mere speech sound from the standpoint of enunciation alone, it is interesting to observe how few people use the tongue and jaw in their speaking, in a manner which insures the maximum of results with the minimum of effort.

In the majority of people, if the speaking voice is pleasing in quality, it is almost always the case that the muscles of the root of the tongue, which involve the throat muscles, are used a very great deal in the production of the spoken word; when in reality it is possible, through the understanding and analysis of vowel and consonant sounds (when released on pure resonance, as in the study of this System), so to minimize the activity in producing the sounds that only the front end of the tongue and the lips are especially active, and move only very slightly to give a clear enunciation, which action brings no resistance.

Vocal tone used with the old idea of muscular placement consciously directs the tone into the frontal cavities; this direction cannot fail to bring with it a state of resistance which dampers resonance, making clear word and tone formation with a minimum of action and without tension impossible.

When we understand that each vocal tone is affected in its production so extremely by the direction of tone to the resonance cavities, and as we realize that the slightest nervous tension in any direction will damper resonance, it can be plainly seen that if the word is spoken clearly with the minimum of action, it will have less effect upon the throat muscles and the formation of the tone in its production in singing. When word sounds are correctly analyzed and carefully released, they are of the *greatest aid* in producing the desired vocal tone; so in going into the explanation of our work in diction as applied to our work in tone production, I cannot lay too much stress upon careful analysis and *comparison* of *vowel* and *consonant* sounds in *every* language. This we find a very great help in our application of syllables to vocal tones, and also of the greatest assistance in our awakening of activity of the inner ear. It is only in our study of word sounds and their combinations that we do any listening during the liberation of the voice—not to the *vocal tones* themselves *at any time* during the study.

Most singers, if they have not made a careful study of diction, produce their word sounds in a more faulty manner than those who do not sing, because the production of vocal tones combined with word sounds, if the word sounds are not made with entire release, are really an obstacle in producing the tones; and because of their being an obstacle the vocal tone has a tendency to pull them toward the back of the tongue, and in so doing the throat muscles become involved and a throaty manner of speaking and singing is the result.

VII

SPONTANEITY AND THE IMPULSE

In my contact with students who are taking this work, the question arises "when and how much one should practice." This point I want to emphasize. *Too much* practice is always harmful in any way of studying. Particularly is it so in *this* way. Stop and consider. What are the principles of this work? Spontaneous activity *first of all;* instantaneous release of tone and vocal sound, without physical sensation; no physical sensation except that of resonance, which is reflected sound-waves. Now your common sense will immediately tell you that even *one* immediate repetition of a tone, a phrase or a release movement will lack the spontaneity gained in doing it for the *first* time. Without the utmost spontaneity our first principle is lacking, so why do it over even twice? Every time we repeat we go farther from spontaneous action and nearer to conscious action and physical sensation. So you see we *cannot* repeat.

You ask, what can we do? We can go from one phase of our work to another. Don't repeat ever. Take another impulse, another tone, another phrase, another movement. In five minutes you can go back and do the first thing again. When you approach it from a fresh viewpoint, then you truly do it with a renewed thought and again we find spontaneity, the Vital Spark.

Our ultimate unfoldment comes from right impressions on the consciousness. Each *right* impression made is a step *ahead;* each *wrong* impression a step *backward.* That is another reason why we cannot afford immediate repetition of anything we do. The moment we repeat a word, a tone, an impulse, we are unconsciously imitating what we have done before, and in so doing losing the vital point in all this work, *Spontaneity.* If we immediately repeat a song or a movement, and it is not quite so good as it was before, we have left an impression less good than the one we might have left if we had quit at the time the tone was at its best. I feel it is most necessary again to emphasize the difference between voluntary (conscious) or automatic action, and spontaneous action.

Conscious (voluntary) action is any action controlled and directed by the conscious mind and will power. Automatic action is action that is first voluntary action and has been made a habit through repetition, and because of its becoming a habit, does not need the constant direction of the conscious mind. It is also wholly mechanized, without real spontaneity.

Spontaneous action is action which is instantaneous and is the result of the activity of the creative impulse. Consequently, when all action used in producing the voice becomes spontaneous, we have no sensation whatever in the production of tone, aside from that of resonance, for without the drive of will power there is no resistance.

When we are in a normal condition, we are never conscious of the act of tone production in speech. It is true there are no sensory nerves connected with the motor nerves which control the production of the voice. It is only when used with will power and resistance that there is sensation. It also proves, when the voice is wholly produced through spontaneous action, that there can be no wear, strain, or fatigue upon the body because of tension. It is only when an artificial mechanized condition is used (that brings into use conscious or automatic action as applied to the production of tone), that the voice becomes tired in speaking or singing.

It is well, then, for the student who is studying this course, to remember that in each step he takes we are constantly striving to retain this condition of spontaneous activity in everything we *think* or *do*. When any action is sensationless we may be quite sure that it is spontaneous. Many teachers of *instrumental* music constantly confuse those two terms, automatic and involuntary action. It may have been repeated many dozens of times to produce this condition, which is not spontaneous but automatic.

When we have learned to drop the tongue and jaw into the unconscious position, and can use it in that manner with no physical sensation, we may consider we are doing this correctly. When one can say with perfect clarity each letter of the alphabet with the jaw and tongue in this condition, he has produced the sounds correctly.

In this detailed analysis of the speech organs and their activity through this form of tone production, much has been said about tongue and jaw and the great necessity of their independent, sensationless activity throughout all phases of this plan of unfoldment. The other speech organs which are equally important, and the activity of which we have as yet only touched upon, are the lips and their movement. In the old manner of vocal usage (which is dependent upon breath and its control, physical effort and will power drive), we have accepted a facial expression which is wholly unnatural and in no way can express the thought the words of the song convey.

The basic reason for this, is the force and resistance that are always used in the production of tone which is associated with breath. In no way is it possible to lay aside the extreme opening and closing of the mouth which is carried on throughout the old form of singing, because as long as the Solar Plexus is associated with the tension of the diaphragm in its support of the breath, the resistance of the jaw in the chewing muscles makes this necessary. Consequently, with almost every syllable uttered the jaw is opened widely for the tone emission. When the jaw is used *in this* manner, the mask of facial muscles which underlie the skin of the whole face, including the lips, is also more or less set in resistance. This makes it impossible for the lips to gain the independent action they are expected to have in natural speech. The opening and closing of the jaw takes the place of the independent lip activity which should play an important part in the facial expression, in singing as well as in speech.

In this manner of tone production (because there is no usage of breath, force, resistance or sensation in any part of the body), the facial muscles can be so released and liberated in their activity over the whole countenance, that the emotional content may be expressed by the singer with all the advantages that the dramatic actor finds in his art.

In our study of the book of vocalises, "Vaccai", we cannot be too careful in knowing our thought is always that of *speaking* the syllable and impulse rather than singing. The thought of speaking when we produce our sounds will always give the minimum of conscious action and the maximum of spontaneous activity, because no habit which may have been wrong in our previous style of singing will trouble us. In the study of these Italian exercises, I wish again to emphasize the necessity of committing them to memory, all of the words—before we are even allowed to study the syllables and impulses *as such.* Commit them to memory by *saying* them rapidly, carefully and clearly, until the tongue, jaw and lips naturally take the positions for the Italian sounds.

When we can read them through fairly well, it is well to consider them as syllables. After we have considered them as syllables, we may begin to study the impulses. It is better, after having analyzed the first and second impulse of each syllable, to dwell entirely upon the release of the first impulse, leaving out the second impulse of the syllable, because all our lives we have been taught to consider the first and second impulses as a unit. Consequently, the whole thought should be given to the release of the initial sound of the syllable (which is the impulse), until we have mastered it.

The study of words, syllables and impulses should all be done at first with no thought of the music. In fact, it is better to have the pupil copy the words of any song or exercise in a little notebook, which he may carry with him and keep his mind entirely away from the *pitches* and notes until this work is accomplished.

In order to study the music of a song or exercise, it is best to learn the time and tune through playing the air. When we have committed the time and tune perfectly, then it is well to go over the time and tune with the words in *conversational* tone. This makes it possible for us to learn the time and the words perfectly before having touched the vocal process of production. When we begin to use the tune without words, our whole thought may be concentrated upon voice production alone. The idea of perfect tone production and clear enunciation should be kept before every student of singing, until he has accomplished it. This is a matter of very great importance for the student to consider, and yet there is another matter of even greater importance.

If most sounds are properly analyzed and *inflection* clearly understood, we find very readily that the right accent of "word sound", consonant, vowel and inflection aids us very materially in the production of musical tone. Consequently, this idea of impulse is of two-fold importance to every student, and too much time or thought cannot be given to the proper analysis of sounds, consonants, vowels and inflection. Inflections are readily heard by the inner ear, where at the *beginning* the outer ear hears only the most prominent sounds.

Consequently, as we work, bit by bit, the inner ear becomes sensitized to the point of hearing previously hidden sounds of words, syllables, vowels, consonants and their inflections. The outer ear has always been associated with the conscious activity and direction of all muscles associated with what is called the vocal and respiratory tract, and with those of the speech organs. The inner ear is associated with all the finer sensibilities and is *connected in no way* with will power direction, muscular action or physical sensation. The *inner* ear is always in perfect tune, and in cases where people are said to be "tone deaf', it is only that the inner ear does not coordinate with the outer or physical ear. The physical or outer ear can only direct the state of perfect tuning through using the inner ear. So, when we are able to *lay aside* the physical *outer* ear, and its reactions (in all our musical association and activity), we have entered into the real musical world of activity, spontaneity and inspiration.

VIII

ANALYSIS OF SONG STUDY

Material

In this Chapter I wish to explain more clearly the reason for using certain material in our work. The best kind of songs to use in the first year's work are songs which may be called "talking" songs, little songs that have a simple melody with which we express the thought. The tempo of the music should be rather rapid. Until we get a long way from the old thought of pitch, it is better to use songs the compass of which extends, we will say, from middle "C" to "C" above the staff. This kind of song is not far away from the natural speaking sound of the voice, which in time we wish to extend through a compass of from two to three octaves. It is much better to study songs which have no dramatic intensity, songs which tell a simple little story in a simple way. Songs of this type may be used in the English and the Italian languages. We never use the French or German languages. Students who are familiar with the English language are very likely to use muscular adjustment in those two languages.

It is best not to use an accompaniment while the student is using his vocal tone, for at least three-fourths of the first year's work, and never in any case until the words, the time, the tune, the impulses, are all perfected. When the voice is ready to use with the accompaniment, we endeavor in every way to apply to every sentence the natural inflection of speaking.

A group of "talking" songs for high voice follows:

"A Winter Lullaby"	*DeKoven*
"A Disappointment"	*Hood*
"An Open Secret"	*Woodman*
"Seeds Song"	*Woodman*
"In Blossom Time"	*Needham*
"Spring Is a Loveable Lady"	*Elliott*

A group of songs for low voice, as follows:

"On the Shore"	*Neidlinger*
"Ashes of Roses	*Wood*
"When Love is Come"	*Speaks*
"Rose in the Bud"	*Forester*
"Gray Days"	*Johnston*
"Absent"	*Metcalf*

When a student is studying a song to learn the impulses perfectly, the time of the song should be reduced to absolutely even notes, each one the same length. That means that each impulse of each syllable should be released in exactly the same way, paying no attention to the time of the song until the impulses are perfected. This enables the student to get an absolutely clear idea of the release of every impulse of each syllable, no matter what the word may be, and it lays aside the feeling of high and low in association with pitch.

The point of using the double consciousness (so-called) in the release of our words and tones should be made very clear in each step of the work. This was explained throughly upon the taking up of the different exercises in "Panofka" and "Vaccai". It is well to keep this point in mind throughout the whole of the work, for it is very elusive and brings the pupil to the understanding of the value of abstract thinking. After having had, all one's life, the feeling that the sustaining of the tones is a matter of direct responsibility in the consciousness of the student, no matter whether the tone is held one count or eight, it is a difficult point to make clear in the pupil's understanding that no matter what the length of the tone in the song he is singing, the detachment of impulses is uniformly instantaneous.

You see, it takes exactly the same amount of time to liberate the tone, if we actually give the right thought to our spoken release of our impulse, whether the tone is going to remain one count or eight counts. The length of the tone for any period of time is dependent entirely upon the tonal balance, for when the tone becomes perfectly balanced this expansion is instantaneous on the release of every impulse.

The thought of the pupil has to be entirely prepared for it along every step of the work, and gradually as the resonance and expansion begin coming into the tones, the pupil will see for himself that after he has released the tone properly it flows on and on through expansion, with seemingly no responsibility on his part except the fact of keeping the condition the same as when it started, and the thought of release during the duration of the tone.

I wish to call attention here to a very strange error that is being made by the publishers of songs of all classes today, that is, the wrong division of words and syllables. For instance, I have seen the word "loving" divided in this manner "Lo" (first syllable), "ving" (second syllable), making the consonant begin the second syllable when it does not belong there. The reason for this has been the indirect influence of singers upon the publishers, in the manner in which they say their words. When a singer's tone is founded upon the support of the breath, it is very much easier to make a syllable clear if that syllable can begin with a consonant. A consonant at the beginning of a syllable enables a singer to give a push to the syllable which, in most cases, makes it more definite when the breath is being used as a support for the tone.

Another word wrongly divided was the word "snowing", being spelled "sno" (first syllable) "wing" (second syllable). Another word, "spirit". The first syllable was given as "spi", the second as "rit". This fault of division of words in printed songs leads to imperfect diction on the part of singers who do not know better; and has come, not through the fault of publishers, but through the demands of wrong singing.

A syllable beginning with a vowel sound is much more dependent upon a perfectly balanced tone (pure resonance) than a syllable beginning with a consonant; consequently, when a singer is trying to sing without being able to use an even scale, viz., (each tone being equally dependent upon a perfectly tuned condition), and his voice is dependent upon breath support, he finds it easier to start each syllable with a consonant, if possible. Observe the words of your song carefully, and first of all make the word divisions absolutely correct according to the rule of English, allowing as many syllables as possible to begin with a vowel.

When each tone of a voice is perfectly in tune and balanced, one language is as easy as another in which to give perfect diction. It does not make any difference what the syllable or what the song, if the student can analyze it clearly before he approaches the sound with tones, he can make any syllable in any language perfectly clear without interfering in any way with the tone production. When syllables begin with vowels it is easier to release the tone. This is the reason that it has always been said that the Italian language is easier to sing than any other, for so many of the sounds are the open vowel sounds. If words and syllables are *not mutilated* in their division, it is also as easy to sing consonants; but when it is possible in any language, allow the syllable to begin with a vowel sound—vowels are an aid to the flow and expansion of resonance.

There is another point that I wish to make clear.

I have spoken several times before of the principle which applies the same to a slur as to a cadenza. It is difficult at first to get the student to understand that if he has a group of two notes to be done with one syllable, he must keep the thought of the first impulse and expansion throughout the *two* tones. He should release the impulse instantly and hear the speech sound clearly upon the beginning of the first note, and then allow the tone to flow and expand in an uninterrupted manner through the second note, before the ending comes. This preserves the same quality throughout both tones, and this principle applies as well to ten notes as two. This is a principle that allows a cadenza to be exactly the same quality from the first note to the last—a point which so few singers seem to understand is necessary, or are able to do. When a student's thought is instantly detached at the begining of each impulse from the syllable, the sound which follows may flow with entire purity throughout a slur of two notes, or a cadenza of twenty—the ending of the syllable sound only coming in on the last note of the cadenza.

The less of the sound of the letters of a syllable which comes into a cadenza on release of the first note, the purer the beauty of tone will be throughout the cadenza; and since the beauty of tone is the great beauty of a cadenza or a slur, it is well to draw this fact to the close attention of the student in every case. This fact allows the pupil to use spontaneous activity and *no* muscular movement through *any number* of tones in a cadenza, and unifies the whole group in a very perfect manner. To do this satisfactorily, however, the pupil should play the cadenza until it is clearly impressed upon his mind as a complete melody.

The careful fundamental work that has been done with "Panofka" in the study of the released tones flowing throughout a phrase or measure, will make all these points come easily when we reach them. If there is any difficulty in any of the advanced work, you may look back to the first two, three or four chapters and find that you have not received a clear understanding of some principle which was made in the beginning.

The next kind of song to be used in our study, after having mastered a number of these "talking" songs which I have given in the list, are the use of songs in which occur small cadenzas, a great many slurs and the beginning of work which requires so-called flexibility. These can be done without *muscular* action, when resonance is established in balance. I shall give a list of these songs, which can be purchased for high or low voice, as necessity requires:

"A Mountain Maiden"	*Schleiffarth*
"An Alpine Rose"	*Smith*
"Swing Song"	*DeKoven*
"You and I"	*Lehmann*
"One Spring Morning"	*Nevin*
"Pastorale"	*From "Rosalind"*
"The Swallows"	*Del'Acqua*
"Gay Butterfly"	*Hawley*

A very important part of our teaching material I consider to be arias, from the operas and oratorios by the Great Masters. Before the end of the first year's work, the student should be started in studying these arias. The edition best suited to our purpose is "Opera Songs for Soprano", edited by the Church Company. These volumes come for all voices and are most excellent for our purpose. Also "Oratorio Songs for Soprano", obtainable for all voices—Church Edition.

IX

CONSTRUCTIVE REPERTOIRE

Material

Because my viewpoint of the study of these masterpieces differs so widely from that of a great many teachers of singing, I feel that it is only fair to my students that they should know exactly my reasons for the study of them.

Most teachers do not give these arias to students until after many years of study, their arguments being that there are so few people who are endowed with temperament and voice and all the attributes of the artist to such an extent that they will ever sing these arias in a finished manner; that it is better not to give them to students who are lacking in these attributes. Now, few of us would ever understand the masterpieces in literature if that same argument were taken in schools and colleges. How few people who study Shakespeare in the many classes of our high schools and colleges ever become noted actors, and yet it is considered a part of the development of the mind and character to be able to analyze, to understand and to appreciate Shakespeare, because he is one of the Great Masters in literature.

The lack of musicianship in our vocal students as a class, is greatly deplored by every one, and yet how is musicianship to be gained unless a student has an incentive to do and understand difficult things because he is studying the masterpieces? He need not be led to believe that he will be a great artist and be able to sing oratorio and grand opera as well as the great artists sing them, because he is making a study of them; but think how much better fitted our audiences would be to appreciate the work of great artists if young students should study the masterpieces of song with exactly the same attitude that school children are taught to study the masterpieces of literature. Then, on the other hand, there are *no* vocalises written that can compare in difficulty of intervals, of time, of style, with the great arias of opera and oratorio. Consequently, because of these two viewpoints, I consider that every student who studies singing at least six months, should begin the study of these masterpieces with the right attitude toward them.

It matters not whether his voice will ever be adequate to bring them to the public notice as an artist, but his mind, heart and soul must be steeped with their beauties and their intricacies in such a way that he will be better developed from the standpoint of musicianship all his life, through having studied them.

In this way of working, also because of the necessity of the wide compass in order to *bring in the two sets of overtones necessary* to balance perfectly and bring to a tuned condition *any* voice, it is difficult for us to find music written which brings in the extremes of high and low notes and the wide compass unless we do use arias from operas and oratorios. Consequently, I feel justified in making all my pupils familiar with all kinds of great masterpieces in vocal literature throughout their study.

The same principle should be applied here that we apply to the singing of songs. The music and words of each one of these arias should be learned perfectly; the time, the tune, the words, before a student may consider that he can even begin to use his voice in the study of them. The impulses should be studied carefully so that each one is perfectly clear, then it is time to reduce the music to the idea of each impulse being instantly detached, until the student can release perfectly every syllable from every pitch throughout the whole number.

We are living in a wonderful age. Students have a great advantage in hearing record reproductions and the radio these days. If a student is studying a certain aria, it is a splendid thing to hear as many different artists sing that aria as possible; then the student will compare and analyze in a very thorough way, and not be so likely to *imitate* the *tone* as though he would hear only one singer do the aria, because tonal imitation is not helpful if the student is working from basic principles.

I shall give a short list of these arias which I find most helpful in bringing the study of opera and oratorio to each voice.

Soprano—*Opera*

Thou Lovely Bird — *David*
From "The Pearl of Brazil"
Polonaise — *Thomas*
From "Mignon"
Caro Nome — *Verdi*
From "Rigoletto"
Elizabeth's Prayer — *Wagner*
From "Tannhauser"
Elsa's Dream — *Wagner*
From "Lohengrin"

Soprano—*Oratorio*

With Verdure Clad — *Haydn*
From "The Creation"
Oh, Had I Jubal's Lyre — *Handel*
From "Joshua"
These Are They Which Came, etc. — *Gaul*
From "The Holy City"
Be of Good Comfort — *Cowan*
From "Ruth"

Tenor—*Opera*

'Tis Love, Ah, 'Tis Love — *Gounod*
From "Romeo and Juliet"
Oh Lola Bianca — *Mascagni*
From "Cavalleria Rusticana"
Cielo e Mar — *Ponchielli*
From "Gioconda"
Spirito gentil — *Donizetti*
From "La Favorita"

Tenor—*Oratorio*

If With All Your Hearts *Mendelssohn*
From "Elijah"
Be Thou Faithful Unto Death *Mendelssohn*
From "St. Paul"
Comfort Ye *Handel*
From "The Messiah"
My Soul Is Athirst For God *Gaul*
From "The Holy City"

Bass—*Opera*

Even Bravest Heart May Swell *Gounod*
From "Faust"
The Sparks Fly Through the Smithy Door *Gounod*
From "Phelemon and Bacchus"
Within These Sacred Bowers *Mozart*
From "The Magic Flute"
Oh, Thou Sublime Sweet Evening Star *Wagner*
From "Tannhauser"

Bass—*Oratorio*

It Is Enough *Mendelssohn*
From "Elijah"
Thus Saith the Lord *Handel*
From "The Messiah"
Oh, God Have Mercy *Mendelssohn*
From "St. Paul"

The People That Walked in Darkness — *Handel*
From "The Messiah"

CONTRALTO—*Opera*

Lieta Signor — *Meyerbeer*
From "Huguenots"
Ah, figliuol! — *Meyerbeer*
From "Il Profeto"
My Heart Is Weary — *Thomas*
From "Nadescha"
Voce di donna o D'angelo — *Ponchielli*
From "Gioconda"

CONTRALTO—*Oratorio*

Oh, Rest In the Lord — *Mendelssohn*
From "Elijah"
But the Lord Is Mindful — *Mendelssohn*
From "St. Paul"
Eye Hath Not Seen — *Gaul*
From "The Holy City"
Oh Thou That Tellest Good Tidings — *Handel*
From "The Messiah"

A word about student's recitals. I believe it is the duty of a teacher of singing, not only to himself and his audience, but to his pupil as well, to make very clear upon the appearance of that pupil, exactly the condition in which he found him at the beginning of his work. This is the only way that the work of any teacher can be truly judged, and it is a fact which is sad to relate, that many teachers of singing take advantage of a beautiful natural voice, and in so doing really present a dishonest front to the public; while in reality some pupil who has no natural ability whatever, has really done work which is far more constructive and which shows far more diligence of both teacher and pupil.

It is only with honest dealing in this type of analysis that we may ever come to the point of attaining an ideal standard in singing, for after all, our work with a singing voice is only to make possible the spontaneous expression of the ideas of the composer. It is only to achieve this result that it becomes worth while to liberate the vocal instrument through the understanding of perfect tuning, reflected to the audience through a liberated form of vocal expression.

Because of the length of time it requires to tune a voice to its best perfection, students are very often allowed to grow into the feeling that it is only the manner in which his tones *sound* that is worth while. It *should* be that through the *tuning* of every tone we are enabled to unfold the mind and soul of a student to the point where he is capable and worthy of expressing the thoughts of the Great Masters of song, in such a way that they may come close to the hearts of his listeners.

X

CREATIVE SINGING—THE ART SUPREME

Singing Plus Character and Intelligence

The most important duty of a singing teacher to his pupil, is that of awakening his mind and thought and character to the point of making him a broad thinker along every line of his study. He must be brought to experience a sympathetic feeling and a kindly interest in humanity at large. He can be taught to see how the study of music may correlate with every other interest in life, and in its ultimate unfoldment and usefulness in all lines of thought and endeavor.

Humanity at large is more interested in music than in any of the great arts. It is always inspiring and uplifting (when rightly used) to every one in all walks of life. It is a wonderful bit of leaven that leavens the whole lump. It can be made the means of understanding the deepest thoughts and emotions. Music, in its broadest sense, is like "the touch of nature that makes the whole world kin". It is the most spiritual of all the arts.

If a teacher of music does not awaken within each one of his pupils a clearer recognition of the brotherhood of mankind, he can consider himself a failure in the splendid opportunity his work has presented to him. The unfoldment of the understanding and the appreciation of good music, is one of the greatest factors in the upbuilding of any character. Music depends upon principles as definite and as far-reaching as those upon which rests life itself. Its form and structure may be understood; its laws may be depended upon as well as any organism of nature. He must be taught to love nature in all her moods as much as though he were going to paint pictures, or chisel beautiful statuary. He should understand that the only excuse any one of us has for living is the possibility of being helpful to humanity, and that the knowledge of music opens up many avenues of helpfulness. If the student of music pursues the study of any branch of the arts with this broader, more humanitarian outlook, he will find within himself a source of unending joy in his work. He will recognize that he may continually *analyze* all music, but never *criticize*.

Analysis, in its broadest sense, is constructive. It is the power of reasoning from cause to effect; it is the discrimination between good and bad; it is the instant recognition of values and their comparison; it is the unfoldment of an understanding which never condemns, which is as keen in the analysis of one's own faults and limitations as of those of another; it is the best means of development of a knowledge that enables a student to hold ultimately only the highest ideals for his own attainments, and to strive continually for his own commendation.

Criticism, in its general usage, is *destructive* always. It limits one's power of recognition of values; it limits the perspective; it dims the vision. It is generally understood that the harshest words of a critic are sometimes the very best tonic a singer should have. This may be true in specific cases, but I believe if every critic had the knowledge of analysis which he might have, his words of commendation or appreciation would be much more helpful and always lead to a constructive result rather than to a destructive one in the mind and consciousness of the artist. *Analysis* enables us to *adjust* our vision, not to imperfect work alone, but to be as fair in our recognition of perfect singing as we are in our recognition of imperfect singing.

A few basic principles clearly explained and exemplified in almost any community would change the appreciation and thought of the individuals toward the work of all singers, and if teachers of music in all lines would endeavor to educate their community to this thought of analysis, their own work and the work of every musician and every student would be aided in the greatest possible manner.

In speaking of a singer's work, we would never say, "This contralto sings better than that contralto"—or, "This bass sings better than that bass". It is always quite safe to say, "I like the singing of this bass better than the other"; that is the true way to express it, for after all it is a matter of personal taste, entirely, whom the singer pleases. If every auditor's personal taste is based upon the *recogni-*

tion of the great principles which underlie the correct use of the voice in singing, then personal taste is a very helpful ally in the recognition of good work. It is usually personal taste based upon complete ignorance of the vocal apparatus and its possibilities in singing, that makes the harshest critics. When an auditor conscientiously analyzes the work of a singer he cannot possibly be harsh, for in the work of every singer there is something to commend, and I most heartily endorse the feeling toward singing that should be basic in the judging of one person by another, as to character and individual attributes. It is best always to look for the good and accent *it,* and to lay aside the recognition of the imperfect as easily and as quietly as possible.

I believe if every musician should take upon himself the responsibility of making clear a very few principles of analysis to his own immediate community, it would in a very short time make a great difference in the appreciation of all audiences toward music. Take, for instance, the matter of understanding the work of different singers. There are a few principles which underlie the singing voice which are easy for everyone to understand. The most important one is this: There are no two voices which sound alike enough for one to be able to compare them merely whether they are alike or not alike. Every voice (if it is liberated through the principles nature intended), has within it an individuality as perfect and as different from every other voice, as the face of the person who sings differs from other faces.

One of the greatest wonders of the world of ours is that, with all the millions of inhabitants, there are no two people exactly alike in looks or temperament. Voices may first be classed as sopranos, contraltos, tenors, basses, baritones. Each of these classes may be sub-divided into lyric, dramatic, robusto, coloratura.

Production is a fundamental principle. Upon production depends compass, timbre, quality, color. The points which are generally misunderstood are those of resonance and sound-waves. These two points also rest on production. A voice may have abundant sound-waves but no resonance to speak of —but a voice cannot have resonance without having had first, sound-waves.

Resonance is a result of a blended and reflected condition of sound-waves. When a singer's production allows the sound-waves to flow freely and the reflective capacity is sufficient, we find the reflected quality of sound-waves, which is resonance, to be absolute and unlimited. Resonance is the result of a perfect blending of the upper and lower overtones and their perfect reflection primarily from the elemental sounding board.

Vibrato is very often confused in the mind of the auditor with pulse. Vibrato is very often found in voices which have ample sound-waves, but which are so constricted in production that instead of the sound-wave being reflected freely through the tone, and keeping it perfectly upon the pitch (through blending), it is shaken from side to side across the pitch by the movement of the vibration which is restricted. When a singer uses vibrato he rarely keeps on the pitch. When vibration is properly reflected into resonance, we find a voice that can never deviate from pitch. When vibration is the result of the regular movement of the vocal cords which produce the sound-waves, and when the larynx, which is the main organ of production, is free in its action, with no limitation and no muscular tension or sensation, we find the perfect sound-waves which, when reflected properly, become resonance and pulse. This condition insures the voice its perfect tuning.

Next we come to the emission of word sounds in singing. This is generally classed as "diction". Diction should cover the study and analysis of letter and syllable sounds in all languages, and their various combinations and inflections. To study the diction of a language successfully, we should first understand the language well through the intellect; then we can approach the analysis of the syllable, and by so doing gain the awakening that is necessary of the inner ear, which distinguishes these finer shades of sounds and inflections and enables the student to reproduce them through his organ of tone production and speech. For if the inner ear is carefully unfolded and the organs of speech are properly liberated in their action, and the student begins with the study of the principles of this diction (which underlies all languages), it is a comparatively easy task to perfect the nicety of diction which any singer would strive for, and which at once bespeaks culture.

Pronunciation and enunciation are two terms which are often confused. Pronunciation proves whether our knowledge of a language is such, that we speak the words and syllables according to the rules of the language; enunciation proves whether our organs of speech are being used in such a manner that we may produce the sounds clearly. Inflection almost touches upon the point of tone color, which in itself, and its adaptation to the singing tone, is very slightly understood by most singers and auditors.

If we liken tone color to the color we find upon the palette of an artist, we may in some measure understand its meaning in regard to expression. Primarily, a tone may be dark or white, so-called. Between these two primary colors lies every varying shade of the rainbow. In the work of a great artist we find the voice so perfectly poised, that every thought and emotion which crosses the mind is reflected in the quality of the tone which is being produced. This is the real true condition that gives us tone color. The difference between the tone color we hear in the work of a great artist and the tone color that is attempted by most singers is this: if the tone production of a singer is limited in any way, it is impossible for him to use his voice in such a manner that his *thought* may be *reflected* in the color of his tone. The only means then left him is to *imitate* as nearly as he can, through the recognition of the sound of the tone color in the voice of an artist, the color he wishes in his own voice. This sort of tone color stands in the same relation to the real tone color that the chromo does to the real painting. In other words, it is merely a cheap imitation of the real thing. That is the main reason that I believe teachers of singing, as a rule, should be more careful than they are in giving ideas of expression and interpretation through *imitation.*

Expression should never be taught by *imitation,* for what we get by imitation can never reflect tone color, truly. The perfection of the vocal instrument should first be attained, then as the vision and imagination of the pupil unfolds to the point of recognition and expression of great thoughts, he is enabled gradually to reflect those thoughts into his tones from the innermost feelings and consciousness. This reflection of the thought into the tone by the great artist, brings to him the true tone color which is the basis of interpretation.

Note: This complete text book appeared in printed form entitled "Vocalized Speech". Copyrighted 1938 by M. Barbereux-Parry.

A Short Resume of Some "Mile-stones" Which Mark the Progress of a Pioneer in a New Field of Research

In 1896 Mme. Parry made the discovery that the region across the back of the human skull, always known in the science of anatomy as the interosseous spaces, and which she calls the elemental sounding board, is the primary source of vocal resonance.

This discovery led her to the understanding with which she adapted voice production to the principles of the stringed instrument, which requires no breath, physical effort or sensation in tone production.

In 1905 she issued a little booklet, "The First Five Years In a New Method of Singing". In 1915 she published a book called, "Vocal Limitation and Its Elimination". In 1920 she issued a textbook of her work in the form of typewritten Bulletins, which, condensed and revised, is now entitled, "Vocalized Speech".

NOTE—BY THE AUTHOR

For over forty years I have diligently sought, in this country and Europe, to find some one who had been following this line of research, or possibly working along parallel lines, with at least a similar advanced vision of voice production. So far my search has been fruitless, and as yet it seems that I stand alone in this field of research. Because of this fact, many statements I make in the analysis of what I have done may seem to bear a note of finality, possibly because of over-emphasis.

To anyone whom I do not know, who has reached logical conclusions along this line of research and is able to gain practical results in their application, I extend my apology and congratulations, hoping I have made clear the fact, which I fully realize, that what I have thus far accomplished is merely touching the hem of the possibilities of the future in this new field of research.

WESTMAR COLLEGE LIBRARY

96927

MT
825
.B25
1979